S0-BDQ-813

Contents

Acknowledgements

I'd like to express my appreciation to Dave Cross for his technical advice and feedback on this book, as well as for his time spent answering questions from the many Perl neophytes on CGI101.COM's discussion boards. Dave has been very generous with his help, and I really can't thank him enough for that.

I'd also like to thank Joshua R. Poulson, who encouraged me to learn Perl in the first place; Brad Roberts, for answering my MySQL questions and for helping administer the CGI101.COM server; Jack Elmy, who designed the original cover; Phil Reed, who helped me solve some color problems with the new cover; Gene Seabolt, who answered my many Quark questions; and Roy Sutton, who nitpicked the final draft for me.

And finally I am extremely grateful to my parents, Cindy and David Hamilton, who have helped me so much with the printing and shipping of books over the last two years.

Introduction

This book will teach you how to develop a Web message board system (or alternately a Web Log) for your Website. CGI experience is required; if you're a beginner, you should work through the examples in the book *CGI Programming 101* before attempting this project.

This project is designed for Perl on Unix. It also requires MySQL (available from http://www.mysql.com), and the Perl modules CGI.pm and DBI.pm. CGI.pm has been part of Perl starting with Perl 5.004; if your system doesn't have it, then you're using a really old (or badly installed) version of Perl, and should upgrade. If your system doesn't already have DBI.pm installed, you can download it from http://search.cpan.org.

This text is a hands-on project; the goal is to teach you how to tie together a number of advanced CGI concepts into one large application. If you are reading this because you want a message board program for your site (and not because you particularly want to *learn* how to develop one), you can download one from any of the various script sites on the Web.

Conventions Used in this Book

All Perl and HTML code will be set apart from the text by indenting and use of a fixed-width font, like so:

```
print "This is a print statement.\n";
```

Each program in the book is followed by a link to its source code:

⊟ Source code: http://www.cgi101.com/advanced/forums/script.txt

In most cases, a link to a working example is also included:

⇨ Working example: http://www.cgi101.com/advanced/forums/demo.html

Getting Connected

If you already have a Unix shell account with your ISP, visit
http://www.cgi101.com/class/connect.html for links to various programs you can use to
connect to your shell account.

If you don't have a shell account, visit http://www.cgi101.com/hosting/ for information
on CGI101's hosting plans. We offer MySQL and all of the Perl modules you'll need to
develop your message board or blog.

1   Site Design and Usability

Before you begin coding a major CGI-driven site like a discussion board, you need to plan your site design first. *Design* includes:

- Identifying your user group(s)
- Defining the tasks each group needs to accomplish
- Breaking down any major tasks into subtasks
- Deciding which language to use
- Addressing usability issues

User Groups

Our message board design will be for two user groups: regular users who can read and post to forums and reply to individual posts, and board admins who can delete messages and create, edit and delete forums.

Tasks

Tasks that message board users will need to be able to perform are:

- View all available forums (and message counts for each forum)
- View all messages in a given forum
- View all messages in a particular thread
- Read individual messages
- Post new messages
- Reply to messages

An optional but nice feature for users is the ability to search the forums.

Tasks that admin users will need to perform are:

- Delete a message (and possibly an entire thread)
- Create new forums
- Delete forums
- Edit forums (description, expire time, etc.)

And finally there should also be a non-CGI script that runs automatically once per day (or on whatever schedule you want) to expire old messages.

Language

The programming language you use is up to you. This same application could be developed in C, PHP, Java, or whatever you prefer... but for this project we're going to use Perl.

Usability

When you're designing pages for the Web, whether they're static pages or CGI-generated message boards, you should consider the usability of your design before you implement it. Consider why people will come to your site and what tasks they will perform there so that you can make those tasks as easy as possible for them. The main usability points we want to meet with our design are:

- To use a simple, graphics-light design that loads quickly on all browsers
- Limit the amount of scrolling or clicking people have to do to read messages
- Make the navigation links convenient to find and use

Comparing Existing Designs

There are a number of message board systems in use on the Web today; you've probably seen and even used some of them. It can help you in your design process to compare other sites and observe the features you like and don't like about them. Let's take a look at some:

Yahoo! Groups (http://groups.yahoo.com) is a combined message board and mailing list system. The Web interface is the message board front end. Messages are displayed by date or thread (user-selectable), with the latest messages appearing at the bottom of the message index listing. Users click on the message subject to view each individual message. You can't read an entire thread on one page - you have to click on each follow-up to read it. (Undoubtedly this was done not to benefit the reader but the advertiser; more page clicks equals more ad impressions.) Yahoo has also started placing ads into the groups, so often the user is forced to view a full page ad, then has to click again to get past the ad and read the message.

Slashdot (http://www.slashdot.org) is another example, though it isn't a regular discussion board. A Slashdot staffer posts a lead-in story, and readers can then post follow-up comments. The reader has a great deal of control over the display of comments, and can choose the "threshold level" (a rating for each comment indicating its usefulness), display (threaded, nested or "flat" - one message after another), and sorting order (newest first, oldest first, or by score). The reader chooses his or her own display preferences then can view all of the comments that meet those criteria, displayed on one page.

GardenWeb (http://forums.gardenweb.com/forums) has a fairly simple forums setup. Thirty message topics are displayed per page, with the newest topics (or those with the newest follow-up posts) appearing at the top of the page. The reader then clicks on the topic link to read the original post along with any follow-ups. All follow-ups appear on a single page, in chronological order (oldest first). The "post new message/follow-up" form appears on the same page as the message index (at the bottom of the page), though this makes quoting the previous message somewhat difficult.

EZBoard (http://www.ezboard.com) is widely used; it displays forums and message threads in a table format. This system allows users to display graphics within their messages, which means a particular message thread can take a while to load if there are many graphics to display.

Database Design

We'll begin this project by first setting up the MySQL database and the tables needed for the message board. First let's review the goals we set up for the board in the previous chapter:

- View all available forums (and message counts for each forum)
- View all messages in a given forum
- View all messages in a particular thread
- Read individual messages
- Post new messages
- Reply to messages

By reviewing these tasks, you should be able to determine the two tables your database will need: a forums table, with information about each forum, and a messages table, with information about each individual message.

The forums table will need to have fields for the following:

- Forum ID, a unique identifier number (the "primary key")
- Forum name - a short character string
- Forum description - a longer character string
- Rank - an integer number for sorting order
- Expire time - an integer number representing the number of days to keep posts in this forum

The rank column is useful when you have several forums and want to sort them in some order other than alphabetical. Expire time will be used for deleting old messages.

You'll need to create a new database (or choose an existing database) for your forum tables. If you have MySQL admin privileges, create the new database by using the command:

```
mysqladmin -p create cgiforum
```

(You can change the database name from "cgiforum" to whatever you like.) If you don't
have admin privileges, ask your sysadmin to do this for you.

You (or your admin) will also need to set up a username and password in the privileges
tables. Here's the MySQL code to add a new user with username "cgiuser" and
password "fnord", and also grant them access to our cgiforum database:

```
mysql -p mysql

insert into user (Host, User, Password) values (
"localhost", "cgiuser", password("fnord"));

insert into db values ("localhost", "cgiforum", "cgiuser", "Y",
"Y", "Y", "Y", "Y", "Y", "Y", "Y", "Y", "Y");

flush privileges;
```

You should choose some other password for your database (other than "fnord"); if you
already entered this, you can change the password by doing:

```
update user set password=password("mynewpassword") where
user="cgiuser";

flush privileges;
```

The number of columns in the db table may vary across different versions of MySQL; if
you get a "Column count doesn't match value count at row 1" error when attempting the
insert into the db table, you can do a "show fields from db" and count the number of
columns. The first three columns (Host, Db, and User) are standard, and you'll want to
add a "Y" for each privilege column that appears in the table.

Once your database is created, you can create the forums table. (If you're still in
MySQL at this point, be sure to type "use cgiforum" to change databases before you
create the new tables.)

```
create table forums(
        id int not null primary key auto_increment,
        name char(80) not null,
        description char(244) not null,
        rank int not null,
        expiretime int not null);
```

You could use either char or varchar for the string columns. Varchar and char are similar types, except that char pads the unused space in a record with blanks, while varchar actually truncates the unused space.

You'll notice that the forum ID field is auto-incrementing. This way, when we insert new posts into the database, we don't have to waste a query finding out what the current max ID is before incrementing it. auto_increment can only be set on an integer field that's also the primary key of the table. Since both of those are true here, we'll use it.

Next you'll need to create the messages table. This table must contain information about each message:

- Message ID, a unique identifier
- Forum - the ID# of the forum this message is in
- Author's name
- Message subject
- E-mail - the author's e-mail address
- Date and time the message was entered
- Author's hostname or IP address (in case we want to block spammers by IP)
- Text of the message
- Thread ID - this allows us to do semi-threading; on follow-up messages, the thread ID will be the message ID of the first message in the thread. (For the first message in the thread, the thread ID will be 0.)

For this table, the message ID, forum ID, and thread ID will all be integer numbers; the remaining columns except for the message text will be character strings, which have a maximum limit of 255 characters. The message text itself will be defined as type TEXT, which in MySQL can be a text value of 0 to 64 kilobytes. For most message board applications this should be plenty; 64K is a lot of text (around 10,000 words).

Here's the MySQL command to create the messages table:

```
create table messages(
        id int not null primary key auto_increment,
        forum int not null,
        author char(255) not null,
        subject char(255) not null,
        email char(255) not null,
        date datetime not null,
        ip char(255) not null,
        message text not null,
        thread_id int not null);
```

Again, the ID field in the message table is auto-incrementing.

Indexing

Unless your table has indexes, when you send a query to MySQL to search for a certain record, it has to look at every record in the table to see if it matches the query. This is inefficient and can be very slow if you have a large table. The solution to this problem is to add indexes for frequently-searched columns in the table.

The primary key of any table is itself an index, so you don't need to create an additional index for that column. Determining which additional indexes you need will depend on knowing what sort of queries you'll be doing. Sometimes you won't really know the various queries you'll be doing until you're well into a project, but you can add indexes after a table is created by using the following MySQL command:

```
create index index_name on table_name (col1);
```

You can also create an index that includes several columns:

```
create index index_name on table_name (col1, col2, col3);
```

Let's review the design tasks again to see where we might need indexes:

1. View all available forums (and message counts for each forum). Since we're selecting all the data from the forums table anyway, there's no need for any extra index there. However, to count all messages in a given forum, we'll be selecting the number of messages in the messages table that match each forum ID, so we'll want an index on the forum column in the messages table.
2. View all messages in a given forum. Again we'll be selecting all messages from the messages table with the forum number of the forum we're viewing. This is the same index needed as for step one.
3. View all messages in a particular thread. Here we'll be selecting messages that have a thread_id that matches the original post's message ID. We'll want an index on the thread_id column.
4. Read individual messages. This only requires querying the database for the message ID of the post being read - and since the message ID is already a primary key, we don't need to add an index.
5. Reply to messages. This is the same as reading, as far as indexes go.
6. Post new messages. You'll have to do a query to get the forum info on the forum being posted to - but again, since the forum ID is already a primary key in the forums table, no extra index is needed.

7. Search the forum. Most searches will be on the content of the posts, so we'll have to add an index on the message column itself.

So, from this you can see that you need indexes on three columns in the messages table: the forum column, the thread_id column and the messages column. You can create the first two like so:

```
create index forum_index on messages (forum);
create index threadid_index on messages(thread_id);
```

You'll also need to index the messages column itself, but since that's a text column, you have to handle it differently. If you define a regular index on a text column, you'll end up with a huge index file that eats up a lot of disk space. So instead, you'll want to use a full-text index. Full-text indexes are new as of MySQL version 3.23.23. Searching columns using a full-text index is done by using the match() function, but we'll cover that in Chapter 10 when we write the actual search code for the forums. For now we'll just add the index. The syntax for creating a full-text index is:

```
create fulltext index index_name on table_name (column1,
column2, etc.)
```

And here is the MySQL to apply this to your already-created message board table:

```
create fulltext index msg_index on messages (message);
```

Now our databases are set up, and we're ready to start writing some actual CGI code.

References:

How MySQL Uses Indexes - http://www.mysql.com/doc/M/y/MySQL_indexes.html

MySQL Full-text Search - http://www.mysql.com/doc/F/u/Fulltext_Search.html

MySQL CHAR and VARCHAR types - http://www.mysql.com/doc/en/CHAR.html

Message Board Module

We'll be writing a separate script for every task in the message board design, so in order to minimize duplicate code, we're going to set up a module for common code that all of the scripts can use. This will include tasks like opening the database handle with DBI, printing headers and footers, and handling errors. As you develop your program, if you notice any other sections of code that you're having to rewrite for several scripts, those would also be good candidates for this module.

To get started, create a new file named MyBoard.pm and enter the following code:

```perl
# the name of this module. Whatever package name you
# use, you should name the file the same name, with
# a .pm extension.
package MyBoard;

# strict is considered good programming style; it
# requires you to declare all variables before using them.
use strict;

# We need the DBI module to talk to MySQL.
use DBI;

# the CGI module
use CGI;

# CGI::Carp module sends warnings and error messages
# to the browser (so we can see them) - use this
# during development only
use CGI::Carp qw(warningsToBrowser fatalsToBrowser);

require Exporter;
@ISA = qw(Exporter);
@EXPORT = qw();
```

Don't quit your editor yet - there's more to add. We'll discuss each section separately.

Now we'll add the shared code. First off, the module itself will be opening the database connection, and passing the database handle to the scripts. So to do that, add this to MyBoard.pm:

```
our $dbh = DBI->connect("dbi:mysql:cgiforum", "cgiuser",
"fnord", { RaiseError => 1, AutoCommit => 1 }) or
&dienice("Can't connect to database: $DBI::errstr");
```

Replace "fnord" with whatever password you used when you created your database.

You'll also need to create an instance of the CGI.pm module:

```
our $cgi = CGI->new;
```

We'll be doing several redirects in the code, so if you set up the URL to your boards as a variable here (instead of hard-coding it into each script), it'll be fairly easy to change later if you ever move your board to another server:

```
our $url = "http://www.cgi101.com/advanced/forums";
```

(You should change this to your own URL.)

Notice the use of our before the declarations of $dbh and $cgi. If you omit this, then the scripts will fail because of the use strict pragma, which requires you to declare all variables (using my, our, or use vars). our makes these variables *package variables* which can be exported, which is what we want. Unfortunately our is only present in Perl 5.6.0 or later (you can type perl -v at your Unix shell prompt to see what version your server has); if you are using an older version, instead of using our you should add a use vars to the declaration section:

```
use vars qw($dbh $cgi);
```

use vars and our do effectively the same thing.

Now we'll add do_header and do_footer. These subroutines handle printing out the HTML header, page title and body tag, and closing </body> and </html> tags. The advantage to doing this in the main module is that you can change the look of your entire board just by modifying these subroutines, rather than having to edit every script. These are pretty barebones right now, but you could get very elaborate with your page design (displaying header logos, formatting the pages inside tables, etc.) and still handle it all from these two subroutines. We're also going to declare another global variable ($has_header) to indicate whether the page header has been displayed or not:

```perl
our $has_header = 0;

sub do_header {
    my($page_title) = @_;
    if ($has_header == 0) {
        print $cgi->header;
        print $cgi->start_html(-title=>$page_title,
                                -bgcolor=>"#ffffff",
                                -text=>"#000000" );
        $has_header = 1;
    }
}

sub do_footer {
    print $cgi->end_html;
}
```

Next we'll add the dienice subroutine, a general catch-all error handler:

```perl
sub dienice {
    my($msg) = @_;
    &do_header("Error");
    print qq(<h2>Error</h2>\n);
    print qq($msg\n);
    &do_footer;
    exit;
}
```

Use my() to enclose any variables created within your subroutines. my() declares the variables (which appeases the use strict pragma) and limits the scope of those variables to the enclosing code block (in this case, the subroutine itself).

You may also want to add a dbdie subroutine. This calls dienice, but it specifically handles database errors:

```perl
sub dbdie {
    my($package, $filename, $line) = caller;
    my($errmsg) = "Database error: $DBI::errstr<br>\n
called from $package $filename line $line";
    &dienice($errmsg);
}
```

dbdie takes advantage of Perl's caller function to get information about the current subroutine call. Using dbdie means you don't have to pass the error string in (it's carried in automatically). dbdie will also show you the line number where the error occurred on, which may be useful for debugging.

Finally, we need to go back to the top of MyBoard.pm and modify either EXPORT_OK or EXPORT to include the names of the subroutines and variables we want to export:

```
@EXPORT = qw(dienice do_header do_footer dbdie $dbh $cgi $url);
```

dienice, dbdie, do_header and do_footer are all subroutine names, but you can also export variables (provided you declared them globally with our or use vars). Here we're exporting the $dbh database handle, the $cgi module instance, and the base $url.

If you use EXPORT_OK, then each individual script that imports the module must specifically list the variables and subroutines to include:

```
use MyBoard qw(dienice do_header do_footer $dbh);
```

If you put everything into EXPORT, then all of the exported variables and subroutines are automatically imported into each script, so all you have to do is:

```
use MyBoard;
```

in each individual script. So, to simplify things, we're going to export everything.

You also need to add this as the very last line of MyBoard.pm:

```
1;
```

This is the same as "return 1;" and returns a true value. If your module doesn't return a true value, an error will be raised on compilation and your scripts won't run at all.

Save your file, and in the Unix shell type chmod 644 MyBoard.pm. The .pm file is not intended to be run directly, so it doesn't need to be executable (mode 755) like all of our other scripts. It just needs to be readable by the Webserver.

Now, as a security measure, you should also create an .htaccess file to prevent snooping visitors from viewing the source of your MyBoard.pm file. If your Webserver is already set up to refuse access to these, then you don't have to worry about it, but if not, you want the added security to keep people from viewing your module code (and more importantly your database password, which is visible in the code).

Create the .htaccess file in the same directory, and enter the following lines:

```
<FilesMatch "\.pm$">
Order deny,allow
Deny from all
</FilesMatch>
```

Save the file, then chmod 644 .htaccess so the server can read it.

Here is the complete source code for MyBoard.pm:

```perl
package MyBoard;
require Exporter;
@ISA = qw(Exporter);
@EXPORT = qw(dienice do_header do_footer dbdie $dbh $cgi $url);
@EXPORT_OK = qw();
use strict;
use DBI;
use CGI;
use CGI::Carp qw(warningsToBrowser fatalsToBrowser);

our $dbh = DBI->connect("dbi:mysql:cgiforum", "cgiuser",
"demivu7", { RaiseError => 1, AutoCommit => 1 }) or
&dienice("Can't connect to database: $DBI::errstr");

# create the instance of CGI.pm
our $cgi = CGI->new;

# URL
our $url = "http://www.cgi101.com/advanced/forums";

our $has_header = 0;

sub do_header {
    my($page_title) = @_;
    if ($has_header == 0) {
        print $cgi->header;
        print $cgi->start_html(-title=>$page_title,
                    -bgcolor=>"#ffffff",
                    -text=>"#000000");
        $has_header = 1;
    }
}
```

```
sub do_footer{
    print $cgi->end_html;
}

sub dienice {
    my($msg) = @_;
    &do_header("Error");
    print qq(<h2>Error</h2>\n);
    print qq($msg\n);
    &do_footer;
    exit;
}

sub dbdie {
    my($package, $filename, $line) = caller;
    my($errmsg) = "Database error: $DBI::errstr<br>\n called
from $package $filename line $line";
    &dienice($errmsg);
}
```

⊟ Source code: http://www.cgi101.com/advanced/forums/MyBoard.txt

Now we can move on to writing scripts that actually do something.

References

Documentation for Perl's `caller` function:
http://www.perldoc.com/perl5.6.1/pod/func/caller.html or `perldoc -f caller`

Viewing All Forums

The first thing a visitor to your forums will see (unless they are coming in via a search engine) will be the "View All Forums" page. This will show them the name and description of every forum, plus a message count for each forum. Before we can do this though, we should set up a new forum in the MySQL database. So, go into MySQL and enter the following command:

```
insert into forums values(1,"General Discussion", "Whatever",
1, 90);
```

This creates a new forum named "General Discussion" with an ID of 1, description of "Whatever", rank of 1 and expire time of 90 days. The rank is irrelevant if you only have one forum, but it'll be important later for sorting multiple forums.

Now the actual script is going to do a simple query to select all of the forums from the forums table. Create the following script and name it index.cgi:

```perl
#!/usr/bin/perl -Tw
# -Tw turns on taint checking and warnings

# be strict, declare variables with my()
use strict;

# include the current directory in the path for searching
# for modules
use lib '.';

# this includes the MyBoard.pm module
use MyBoard;

&do_header("Forums");
```

```
print qq(<h2>My Forums</h2>\n);

my($sth) = $dbh->prepare("select * from forums order by rank,
name") or &dbdie;
my($rv) = $sth->execute;
my($f);
while ($f = $sth->fetchrow_hashref) {
    print qq(<b><a href="forum.cgi?forum=$f->{id}">
$f->{name}</a></b> - $f->{description}<p>\n);
}

&do_footer;
```

⊟ Source code: http://www.cgi101.com/advanced/forums/ch4index.txt
⇨ Working example: http://www.cgi101.com/advanced/forums/ch4index.cgi

Save and "chmod 755" the script, then call it up in your Web browser.

This doesn't display message counts, but we'll get to that in a moment. The select is ordered first by rank, then by name. This lets you control the order the forums appear on this page by adjusting the rank value. Rank 1 forums appear before rank 2, etc.

The loop itself formats the forum info for display. You can change the display of this page by modifying the print statement statement inside the while loop.

Displaying Message Counts

Our basic script only displayed the forum names and descriptions. But we also want to get the message counts in each forum. You could do a second select inside the while loop to get this data. This isn't terribly efficient though. A better choice is to use a LEFT JOIN in your initial query. A left join selects data ("select *") from two tables at once ("from tableA left join tableB"), matching on a particular field ("on tableA.field = tableB.field"). Unlike a regular join, a left join returns data from the first table even when there are no matching rows in the second table:

```
select forums.id, name, description, count(messages.id) as
msgcount from forums left join messages on forums.id =
messages.forum group by forums.id order by rank, name;
```

This will select the ID, name, and description of every record in the forums table, plus the number of messages in each forum (even if that number is zero).

And, it only requires a slight adjustment to your original code:

```
my($sth) = $dbh->prepare("select forums.id, name,
description, count(messages.id) as msgcount from forums left
join messages on forums.id = messages.forum group by forums.id
order by rank, name") or &dbdie;
my($rv) = $sth->execute;
my($f);
while ($f = $sth->fetchrow_hashref) {
        my($msg) = "message";
        if ($f->{msgcount} != 1) {
            $msg .= "s";
        }
        print qq(<b><a href="forum.cgi?forum=$f->{id}">
$f->{name}</a></b> ($f{msgcount} $msg) -
$f->{description}<p>\n);
    }
```

⊟ Source code: http://www.cgi101.com/advanced/forums/index.txt
⇨ Working example: http://www.cgi101.com/advanced/forums/index.cgi

Note that we didn't have to specify "forums.name" or "forums.description" in the select, like we did with "forums.id". This is because the name and description fields exist only in the forums table, whereas the ID field exists in both the forums table and the messages table. When there's a conflict, you have to specify which table you want the data from.

From a usability standpoint, if you only have one forum on your discussion board, it's better to skip the forums listing entirely and jump right into the message listing for that forum. To modify your script to do this, you'll want to count the number of forums before displaying the page header with do_header:

```
$sth = $dbh->prepare("select count(*), max(id) from forums") or
&dbdie;
$rv = $sth->execute;
($fct, $fid) = $sth->fetchrow_array;
if ($fct == 1) {
    print $cgi->redirect("$url/forum.cgi?forum=$fid");
    exit;
}
&do_header("Forums");
```

You may want to wait to add this until you've actually written the forum.cgi script.

A Note About my()

You'll note that we've added `my()` around any newly declared variables in the script. Another way you can handle this is to predeclare all your variables at the start of your script:

```
my($sth, $rv, $f, $asth, $maxct, $msg);
```

Then you don't have to use a bunch of `my()` wrappers inside the code. `my()` actually limits the scope of a variable to the enclosing *code block*, so for example, if you have something like:

```
if ($ENV{QUERY_STRING} eq "foo") {
    my($tmp) = 1;
} else {
    my($tmp) = 0;
}
```

This limits the scope of $tmp to the if-block *only*. If you try to refer to the variable $tmp later in your program, it won't work, because Perl thinks $tmp hasn't been defined.

Of course, you could avoid these problems entirely by not using the `use strict` pragma... but that's not considered good programming style.

References

MySQL's JOIN syntax - http://www.mysql.com/doc/J/O/JOIN.html

Viewing All Messages
in a Forum

Now we want to display all of the messages in a forum. This script will usually be called with a query string in the URL, like so:

```
http://www.yourhost.com/forums/forum.cgi?forum=2
```

The forum ID is accessed using CGI.pm's `param` function:

```
$forum_id = $cgi->param('forum');
```

You could also access the forum ID through the `$ENV{QUERY_STRING}` variable, which is set to everything after the question mark (?) in the URL. Whether you use `$ENV{QUERY_STRING}` or `param` is largely a matter of personal preference, but in general it's better to use `param` if you expect to have more than one variable passed through the query string. The forum.cgi script will initially only have one variable (the forum ID) in the query string, but we'll be adding some extra variables later on to determine how many messages appear on the page, so we'll go ahead and use `param` to retrieve the query string variables in this script.

You'll need to untaint this data, which can be done pretty easily by a regular expression match to ensure that the ID is a numeric value:

```
if ($cgi->param('forum') =~ /^(\d+)$/) {
    $forum_id = $1;
} else {
    &dienice($cgi->param('forum') . " isn't a valid forum
number.");
}
```

After getting the untainted forum ID, all that's left (more or less) is to select all of the messages in this forum. The actual SQL query for this is:

```
select * from messages where forum_id=$forum_id and thread_id=0
order by date desc;
```

This selects all messages which are *original* posts (not follow-ups), and orders them by date in descending order (that means the newest posts appear at the top of the page). You could reverse that ("order by date asc") if you wanted the oldest posts to appear first.

Start a new file named forum.cgi, and enter the following code:

```perl
#!/usr/bin/perl -Tw
use strict;
use lib '.';
use MyBoard;

# declare variables
my($forum_id, $sth, $rv, $f, $count);

# here we untaint the query string
if ($cgi->param('forum') =~ /^(\d+)$/) {
    $forum_id = $1;
} else {
    &dienice($cgi->param('forum') . " isn't a valid forum
number.");
}

# get the name & info on this forum from the forums table
$sth = $dbh->prepare("select * from forums where id=$forum_id")
or &dbdie;
$rv = $sth->execute;
$f = $sth->fetchrow_hashref;
&do_header("$f->{name} Forum");
print qq(<h2>$f->{name} Forum</h2>\n);
print $f->{desc};

# fetch the individual messages in the forum, and
# display the info.
$count = 0;
$sth = $dbh->prepare("select * from messages where
forum=$forum_id and thread_id=0 order by date desc") or &dbdie;
$rv = $sth->execute;
while ($f = $sth->fetchrow_hashref) {
```

```
    print qq(<b><a href="message.cgi?$f->{id}">
$f->{subject}</a></b> ($f->{author})<br>\n);
        $count = $count + 1;
    }

    if ($count == 0) {
        print qq(No messages.<p>\n);
    }

    &do_footer;
```

⊟ Source code: http://www.cgi101.com/advanced/forums/ch5forum.txt
⇨ Working example: http://www.cgi101.com/advanced/forums/ch5forum.cgi?forum=1

Save and "chmod 755" the file, then call it up in your browser. It should read "No messages" since you haven't posted anything yet.

Add Navigation Links

You'll need to add some links to the page to allow people to post new messages and search the forum. This is best done with a subroutine:

```
sub do_nav {
    print qq(<hr><center>\n);
    print qq(<p><a href="newmsg.cgi?$forum_id">Compose
        New Message</a> | );
    print qq(<a href="search.cgi?$forum_id">Search this
        Forum</a></p> );
    print qq(</center><hr>\n);
}
```

You can then add a call to &do_nav to forum.cgi; ideally both before and after the while loop. It may make your page look a bit cluttered now, but once your forums have a lot of posts in them, it'll be more convenient for users if the links appear both at the top and bottom of the message listings.

⊟ Source code: http://www.cgi101.com/advanced/forums/ch5forum2.txt
⇨ Working example: http://www.cgi101.com/advanced/forums/ch5forum2.cgi?forum=1

We'll be returning to forum.cgi later in the text to add some enhancements, but for now let's move on to posting new messages.

Posting a New Message

Posting a message consists of two scripts: an input form, and the script to parse the form data and load it into the database. The input form is fairly straightforward - you just need input fields for the poster's name, e-mail address, message subject and message text.

We're using a CGI script to generate the form (instead of a plain HTML page) because we need to query the database for info about the forum this message is going to be posted to (and to be sure the user isn't trying to post to a nonexistent forum).

Start a new file named newmsg.cgi:

```perl
#!/usr/bin/perl -Tw
use strict;
use lib '.';
use MyBoard;

# declare variables
my($forum, $sth, $rv, $id, $name, $desc);

# untaint the query string
if ($ENV{QUERY_STRING} =~ /^(\d+)$/) {
    $forum = $1;
} else {
    &dienice("$ENV{QUERY_STRING} isn't a valid forum
    number.");
}

# get the forum info
$sth = $dbh->prepare("select * from forums where id=?");
$rv = $sth->execute($forum);
```

```
my($f) = $sth->fetchrow_hashref;
&do_header("New Topic in $f->{name}");


print <<EndForm;
A valid e-mail address is required to post a message here.<p>

<form action="postmsg.cgi" method="POST">
<input type="hidden" name="forum" value="$forum">
<pre>
Your Name:      <input type="text" name="name" size=40>
Email Address: <input type="text" name="email" size=40>
Subject:        <input type="text" name="subject" size=40>
</pre>
Enter your message below. Do not use HTML tags.<p>
<textarea name="message" rows=10 cols=78
wrap="HARD"></textarea>
<p>
<input type="submit" value="Post Message">
<input type="reset" value="Erase">
</form>


EndForm

&do_footer;
```

⊟ Source code: http://www.cgi101.com/advanced/forums/newmsg.txt
⇨ Working example: http://www.cgi101.com/advanced/forums/newmsg.cgi

Save and "chmod 755" the file. Now you should be able to click on the "Compose New Message" link from your forums.cgi page and get to the input form.

Next you need a script to parse the form data. We're going to use CGI.pm to do the actual decoding, so all that's really involved here is verifying that the form input is valid, and inserting the data into the database.

Start a new file called postmsg.cgi:

```
#!/usr/bin/perl -Tw
use strict;
use lib '.';
use MyBoard;
```

```
my($forum, $sth, $i);

# do some error-checking - be sure they filled out all fields
# $cgi->param() with no arguments returns an array of the
# input field names.
foreach $i ($cgi->param()) {
    if ($cgi->param($i) =~ /^\s*$/) {
        &dienice("$i was blank - please fill out all of the
fields.");
    }
}

$forum = $cgi->param('forum');

$sth = $dbh->prepare("insert into messages(forum, author,
subject, email, date, ip, message, thread_id)
values(?,?,?,?, current_timestamp(), ?,?,?)") or &dbdie;

$sth->execute($cgi->param('forum'), $cgi->param('name'),
$cgi->param('subject'), $cgi->param('email'), $ENV{REMOTE_ADDR},
$cgi->param('message'), 0) or &dbdie;

print $cgi->redirect("$url/forum.cgi?$forum");
```

⊟ Source code: http://www.cgi101.com/advanced/forums/ch6postmsg.txt

Save the file and "chmod 755" it, then try posting a message. If all goes well, you should be returned to the forum.cgi page and see your message displayed there.

As you can see, we haven't done much in the way of data validation, other than to be sure the message isn't empty. Additional checks that should be done are:

- Verifying the poster's e-mail address
- Stripping out any HTML tags from the subject and author's name
- Optionally stripping out any HTML in the message

You can validate the poster's e-mail address by using the regular expression code we developed in Chapter 14 of *CGI Programming 101*:

```
if ($cgi->param('email') !~ /[\w\-]+\@[\w\-]+\.[\w\-]+) {
    &dienice("You didn't enter a valid e-mail address.");
}
```

Add this to your script in the error-checking section - before you write anything to the database, of course.

Removing HTML

You definitely don't want HTML to appear in the subject line (OR in the author's name) because a malicious poster could insert a `<script>` tag and run some Javascript to hijack visitors' browsers. Whether you allow HTML in the message body is up to you - you should certainly filter out any `<script>` tags, but there are a number of other tags which could seriously alter the output of your messages, so it may be easier to remove all tags.

You can delete HTML tags completely by using the following code:

```
my($subject) = $cgi->param('subject');
$subject =~ s/\<[^\>]*>//g;
```

This won't match tags that wrap across line breaks, however. You might get around it by stripping out all the line breaks before you remove the tags:

```
my($message) = $cgi->param('message');
$message =~ s/\n//g;
$message =~ s/\<[^\>]*>//g;
```

However this isn't very neat either. It'll disrupt any special formatting the poster intended to have, for example if they posted a sample of code, or a poem, where line breaks are important.

You could also substitite anything that looks like a tag with its respective HTML character code. The code for a less than sign (<) is < and the code for the greater-than sign (>) is > - so if you substitute these, then you've removed any dangerous HTML:

```
$message =~ s/</&lt;/g;
$message =~ s/>/&gt;/g;
```

You could also filter out HTML tags by using a module designed for that purpose.

Perl Modules

One of Perl's strongest features is the ready availability of modules - code that others have already written and freely contributed to CPAN (the "Comprehensive Perl Archive Network") for sharing with the rest of the Perl community. In a case like this, it'll probably be better to use a module to filter HTML in your message posts, rather than coding your own.

Visit http://search.cpan.org/ and search for "remove HTML tags". You'll get a lot of results, which may look something like this:

1. **HTML::TagFilter**
   An HTML::Parser-based selective tag remover
   HTML-TagFilter-0.07 - 25 Oct 2001 - William Ross

2. **HTML::TagReader**
   Perl extension module for reading html/sgml/xml files by tags.
   HTML-TagReader-0.10 - 13 Aug 2002 - Guido Socher

3. **PerlPoint::Tags::HTML**
   PerlPoint tag set used by pp2html
   PerlPoint-Converters-1.01 - 21 Dec 2001 - Lorenz Domke

4. **PerlPoint::Tags::SDF**
   PerlPoint tag set used by pp2sdf
   PerlPoint-Package-0.37 - 27 Apr 2002 - Jochen Stenzel

5. **PerlPoint::Tags**
   processes PerlPoint tag declarations
   PerlPoint-Package-0.37 - 27 Apr 2002 - Jochen Stenzel

(etc.)

The results consist of the module name (which is a link to documentation about that module), a brief description of the module, a link to the module's download page, the date the module was last updated, and the author's name (which is a link to other modules contributed by the same author). You may have to read through the documentation on various modules to find one appropriate for the task at hand.

From this list we see HTML::TagFilter is probably the best candidate:
http://search.cpan.org/doc/WROSS/HTML-TagFilter-0.07/TagFilter.pm

This module requires HTML::Parser, so you'll have to install both of them if they're not already present on your system. You can see if they're already installed - and read the documentation on them - by typing `perldoc HTML::Parser` and `perldoc HTML::TagFilter` at the shell prompt. If you get a "No documentation found" message, then the module probably isn't installed. A surefire way to see if a module is installed is to type this at the shell command line:

```
perl -e "use HTML::Parser;"
```

If the module isn't installed, you'll get an error saying "Can't locate HTML/Parser.pm in @INC".

You can download the TagFilter and Parser modules here:

```
http://search.cpan.org/search?dist=HTML-TagFilter
http://search.cpan.org/search?dist=HTML-Parser
```

Download the .tar.gz file for each module. (If you download it to your PC first, you'll have to upload it to your Unix server; be sure to use binary mode for the transfers.) Once downloaded, you can unpack the modules in the Unix shell by typing:

```
gzip -d HTML-TagFilter-0.07.tar.gz
tar -xvf HTML-TagFilter-0.07.tar
cd HTML-TagFilter-0.07
```

At this point, installation consists of these commands:

```
perl Makefile.PL
make
make test
make install
```

You will not be able to `make install` unless you have root privileges on your system. If you don't have root, you can leave the module in whatever directory you built it in - or you can copy the .pm file to another directory that you own. (It should not be placed in your Web space, however, because it isn't a CGI script.) For example, let's say you create your own directory for modules in `/home/username/perlmods`. Then to include a module stored in that subdirectory, you can add this to the top of your postmsg.cgi script:

```
use lib '/home/username/perlmods';
use HTML::TagFilter;
```

The use lib line is only needed if you don't have the module(s) available system-wide.

Next you create an instance of the TagFilter module:

```
my($tf) = HTML::TagFilter->new;
```

By default, TagFilter allows some tags, which may or may not be what you want. To remove them all, you clear the list of allowed tags like so:

```
$tf->allow_tags();
```

Now you can strip HTML tags out of the subject line, author name and messages by adding the following to your script:

```
my($subject) = $tf->filter($cgi->param('subject'));
my($message) = $tf->filter($cgi->param('message'));
my($from) = $tf->filter($cgi->param('name'));
```

Be sure to taint-check the e-mail address also:

```
if ($cgi->param('email') !~ /[\w\-]+\@[\w\-]+\.[\w\-]+) {
    &dienice("You didn't enter a valid e-mail address.");
}
```

You could also download and install the Email::Valid module from CPAN, and use it instead of the above code to validate e-mail addresses.

And finally, change the database insert line to use the filtered variables:

```
$sth->execute($cgi->param('forum'), $from, $subject,
$cgi->param('email'), $ENV{REMOTE_ADDR}, $message, 0)
or &dbdie;
```

References

HTML::TagFilter documentation -
http://search.cpan.org/doc/WROSS/HTML-TagFilter-0.07/TagFilter.pm

The Email::Valid module -
http://search.cpan.org/author/MAURICE/Email-Valid-0.14/Valid.pm -

7 Reading Individual Messages

Now that you've posted a message or two, you need to be able to read them. This is a simple script; all you have to do is fetch the message data from the database and display it. You'll also need to either display all of the follow-up messages, or links to the follow-ups. For this project we'll be displaying the follow-ups themselves along with the original message.

Start a new script called message.cgi. The first part looks much like our other scripts:

```perl
#!/usr/bin/perl -Tw
# standard first four lines...
use strict;
use lib '.';
use MyBoard;

my($msgid, $sth, $rv, $count, $msg, $resp);

# untaint the query string
if ($ENV{QUERY_STRING} =~ /^(\d+)$/) {
    $msgid = $1;
} else {
    &dienice("$ENV{QUERY_STRING} isn't a valid message
number.");
}
```

Next we get the message and forum info from the respective tables. Here we have MySQL format the date to more readable format using MySQL's date_format function. We're also grabbing the forum name from the forums table, as well as all follow-ups to the initial message, using a single query. If the number of rows returned ($rv) is zero, then the message doesn't exist, and we'll raise an error:

```
$sth = $dbh->prepare("select messages.*,
date_format(date,'%c/%e/%Y %r') as nicedate, forums.name from
messages, forums where messages.forum = forums.id
and (messages.id=? or thread_id=?) order by thread_id, date")
or &dbdie;
$rv = $sth->execute($msgid, $msgid);
if ($rv < 1) {
    &dienice("Message $msgid does not exist.");
}
$msg = $sth->fetchrow_hashref;
&do_header("Message #$msgid: $msg->{subject}");
print qq(<b><a href="forum.cgi?$msg->{forum}">
$msg->{name}</a> Topic: $msg->{subject}</b><br>\n);
```

Now we can display the message. Since we'll also be displaying the follow-ups on the same page, it makes the most sense to put the display code into a separate subroutine. We've done that here by calling the showpost subroutine, and simply passing the message hashref into it:

```
&showpost($msg);
```

Since $msg is a hashref, and hashrefs are scalar values, you can pass it through to the subroutine like you would any other scalar. One thing to note, though... if you modify any of the values in the hashref *inside* the subroutine, the values will be changed for the original hashref. Since we're not going to be changing anything, though, we won't worry about that here.

Next we look for any follow-ups to the original post, and display them the same way:

```
print qq(<hr noshade>\n);
if ($msg->{thread_id} == 0) {
    $resp = 0;
    while ($msg = $sth->fetchrow_hashref) {
        if ($resp == 0) {
            print "<b>Responses:</b><br>\n";
            $resp = 1;
        }
        &showpost($msg);
    }
} else {
    print qq(This is a followup to another thread. <a
href="message.cgi?$msg->{thread_id}">Click here</a> to view the
entire thread.<br>\n);
```

```
    }
    print "<hr>\n";
    &do_footer;
```

And finally, the showpost subroutine takes the hashref of the message and formats the data for display on the Web page. Notice that we're adding a <br> tag to the end of each line of the message; this allows the message to be displayed more or less as the user typed it.

```
sub showpost {
    my($hdr);
    my($msg) = @_;

    # change all carriage returns to the HTML-ized
    # "break" tag
    $msg->{message} =~ s/\n/<br>\n/g;

    print <<EndHTML;
<hr>
<blockquote>
Message #$msg->{id}<br>
Subject: <b>$msg->{subject}</b><br>
Author: $msg->{author}<br>
Posted: $msg->{nicedate}<br>
<p>
$msg->{message}
</p>
</blockquote>
<font size=-1><a href="reply.cgi?$msg->{id}">Reply to this
post</a></font><p>
<p>
EndHTML
    }
```

⊟ Source code: http://www.cgi101.com/advanced/forums/message.txt
⇨ Working example: http://www.cgi101.com/advanced/forums/message.cgi

And that's all there is to it. Save the file, "chmod 755" it, then try it out in your browser.

References

MySQL `date_format` function -
http://www.mysql.com/doc/en/Date_and_time_functions.html#IDX1293 or
MySQL (Paul DuBois/New Riders), page 537-538

Replying to Messages

At this point you'll want to be able to reply to messages posted on the forums. Start by copying newmsg.cgi over to a new file named reply.cgi. This will save you some typing, because we're only going to modify a few things for posting replies. The first part of the script remains the same:

```
#!/usr/bin/perl -Tw
use strict;
use lib '.';
use MyBoard;

# declare variables
my($msgid, $sth, $rv, $msg, $quotemsg, $subject, $i);

# untaint the query string
if ($ENV{QUERY_STRING} =~ /^(\d+)$/) {
    $msgid = $1;
} else {
    &dienice("$ENV{QUERY_STRING} isn't a valid message
    number.");
}
```

Instead of getting the forum record, we want the record of the message being replied to.

```
# get the message data
$sth = $dbh->prepare("select *, date_format(date,
'%c/%e/%Y %r') as nicedate from messages where id=?") or
&dbdie;
$rv = $sth->execute($msgid);
$msg = $sth->fetchrow_hashref;
&do_header("Reply to Message #$msgid: $msg->{subject}");
```

We want to create a quoted message for the user to reply to. They can delete this from the form field if they wish, but this allows them to easily quote specific text from the original message. We split each line of the message on the line break (\n), then prepend a ">" to the beginning of each line.

```
$quotemsg = qq(At $msg->{nicedate}, $msg->{author} wrote:\n);
foreach $i (split(/\n/,$msg->{message})) {
    $quotemsg .= qq(> $i\n);
}
```

Similarly, we want to include the subject of the original line in the follow-up's subject, however we need to change any quotes (") to the HTML entity for a quote (") so that the quotes don't interfere with the form itself.

```
$subject = $msg->{subject};
$subject =~ s/\"/&quot;/g;
```

The rest of the script is much like newsmg.cgi, except we're going to add a hidden field containing the message ID of the message being replied to, insert the subject line into the value= part of the subject field, and add $quotemsg to the message textarea:

```
print <<EndForm;
A valid e-mail address is required to post a message here.<p>

<form action="postmsg.cgi" method="POST">
<input type="hidden" name="forum" value="$msg->{forum}">
<input type="hidden" name="replyto_id" value="$msg->{id}">
<pre>
Your Name:      <input type="text" name="name" size=40>
Email Address: <input type="text" name="email" size=40>
Subject:        <input type="text" name="subject" size=40
value="Re: $subject">
</pre>
Enter your message below. Do not use HTML tags.<p>
<textarea name="message" rows=10 cols=78 wrap="HARD">
$quotemsg
</textarea>
<p>
<input type="submit" value="Post Message">
<input type="reset" value="Erase">
</form>
EndForm
&do_footer;
```

Next we need to edit postmsg.cgi to allow for posting replies in addition to new messages; the only difference between posting a new message and a reply is the thread_id column in the database. The `prepare` statement can remain the same:

```
$sth = $dbh->prepare("insert into messages(forum, author,
subject, email, date, ip, message, thread_id) values(?,?,?,?,
current_timestamp(),?,?,?)") or &dbdie;
```

Now we wrap an if-else block around the actual database insert. If someone is posting a *new* message, the form will not have the replyto_id field, and so the `param` for it will be blank. Follow-up messages will have the replyto_id field set to the ID of the message they're replying to. You'll have to get the record for *that* message as well, before inserting the reply into the database.

```
if ($cgi->param('replyto_id') eq "") {
# it's a NEW message

    $sth->execute($cgi->param('forum'), $from, $subject,
$cgi->param('email'), $ENV{REMOTE_ADDR}, $message, 0) or
&dbdie;

} else {
# it's a followup; get the info on the message
# being replied to

    $asth = $dbh->prepare("select * from messages where id=?");
    $rv = $asth->execute;
    my($replyto) = $asth->fetchrow_hashref(
$cgi->param('replyto_id'));
    my($thread_id);
    if ($replyto->{thread_id} == 0) {
        $thread_id = $replyto->{id};
    } else {
        $thread_id = $replyto->{thread_id};
    }
    $sth->execute($cgi->param('forum'), $cgi->param('name'),
$subject, $cgi->param('email'), $ENV{REMOTE_ADDR},
$message, $thread_id) or &dbdie;
}
```

Save your script, "chmod 755", and try posting some replies to your previous test messages.

Notice we're using a different database handle ($asth) to get the record for the message that's being replied to; if you were to use $sth, you would overwrite the prepare statement that's already set up to insert the reply into the database. Also, the thread_id is going to be the message ID of the *original* message in the thread. If you're replying to the original message (whose thread_id is 0), then the thread_id is the same as the original message's message_id, but if you reply to a *reply*, then the thread_id is that reply's thread_id.

Here's an example:

ID	Subject	Thread_ID
1	Attack of the Fnords	0
2	Re: Attack of the Fnords	1
3	What's a Fnord?	0
4	Re: Attack of the Fnords	1
5	Re: Attack of the Fnords	1
6	Fnords Rule!!	0

In this example, messages 1, 3, and 6 are new (original messages), and 2, 4 and 5 are follow-ups to message 1. Even if message 5 is a reply to message 4, the thread_id for both of them is still 1. This way the entire thread can be displayed on the single message page, so if you go to message.cgi?1 - it will show message number 1, then all messages with a thread_id of 1, in order.

There are other ways you could thread messages, of course; this is just one simple way. If you were to make your boards fully threaded (where each reply has a thread_id of the actual message number being replied to), it would be much more complex, and may require a large number of database queries to find every follow-up. With our way (single threaded), only a single query is needed to fetch the entire thread.

E-Mailing Replies

A nice feature to have on a message board is the ability to e-mail a reply back to the original poster. Since the original poster may not return to the board to see any replies, e-mail is one way to be sure that person will get your response (assuming they provided a valid e-mail address).

Modify your reply.cgi script and add these lines to the <form> just before the <textarea> tag:

```
<input type="checkbox" name="post" value="1" checked> Post to
boards
<input type="checkbox" name="mail" value="1"> E-mail to
$msg->{author}
```

Save the file. Now edit postmsg.cgi again. We're going to add a test for post vs. mail in the else block:

```
} else {
# this part hasn't changed...
    $asth = $dbh->prepare("select * from messages where id=?");
    $rv = $asth->execute;
    my($replyto) = $asth->fetchrow_hashref(
$cgi->param('replyto_id'));
    my($thread_id);
    if ($replyto->{thread_id} == 0) {
        $thread_id = $replyto->{id};
    } else {
        $thread_id = $replyto->{thread_id};
    }
  # here we test for post vs. mail
    if ($cgi->param('post') eq "1") { # post reply
        $sth->execute($cgi->param('forum'),
            $cgi->param('name'), $subject,
            $cgi->param('email'), $ENV{REMOTE_ADDR},
            $message, $thread_id) or &dbdie;
    }
    if ($cgi->param('mail') eq "1") { # mail reply
        $message = qq(This is a private email reply to your
post on the discussion board at
$url/forum.cgi?forum=$replyto->{forum}.\n\n) . $message;
        &sendmail($cgi->param('email'), $replyto->{email},
            $subject, $message);
    }
}
```

And finally you need to add a sendmail subroutine. If you're only going to be sending mail in this script, then you can put this subroutine inside postmsg.cgi. If you anticipate sending mail from other places, then it'd be a good idea to put it in MyBoard.pm and export it to the scripts that need it. Note we're declaring the $ENV{PATH} environment variable (this is a global variable in Perl so it doesn't need a my() around it); if you

don't define the PATH then you'll get a taint error about an insecure $ENV{PATH}. Be
sure to set the path to include the directory path where sendmail is located (e.g. if
sendmail is in /usr/sbin/sendmail, you'd better include /usr/sbin in the path).

```
sub sendmail {
    my($from, $to, $subject, $message) = @_;
    $ENV{PATH} = "/usr/sbin:/usr/bin";
    my($mailprog) = "/usr/sbin/sendmail -t -oi";
    open(MAIL,"|$mailprog") or &dienice("Couldn't access
$mailprog: $!");
    print MAIL "To: $to\n";
    print MAIL "From: $from\n";
    print MAIL "Subject: $subject\n\n";
    print MAIL $message;
    close(MAIL);
}
```

🖫 Source code: http://www.cgi101.com/advanced/forums/postmsg.txt

If your server doesn't have the sendmail program, you may want to check out the
nms_sendmail script at http://nms-cgi.sourceforge.net/scripts.shtml. This is a drop-in
replacement for sendmail and only requires an SMTP server to connect to.

Tidying Up forum.cgi

At this point we need to go back and modify forum.cgi so it will show the number of follow-ups to each message, along with the date of the most recent follow-up. We're also going to limit the number of topics displayed per page, so if your forum gets very busy, it won't take forever for the page to load.

Show Follow-up Counts

We'll start by displaying the number of follow-ups to each message.

Edit forum.cgi. The first part of the script will remain the same:

```perl
#!/usr/bin/perl -Tw

use strict;
use lib '.';
use MyBoard;

my($forum_id, $sth, $rv, $f, $count);

# here we untaint the query string
if ($cgi->param('forum') =~ /^(\d+)$/) {
    $forum_id = $1;
} else {
    &dienice($cgi->param('forum') . " isn't a valid forum
number.");
}

# get the name & info on this forum from the forums table
```

```
$sth = $dbh->prepare("select * from forums where id=$forum_id")
or &dbdie;
$rv = $sth->execute;
$f = $sth->fetchrow_hashref;
&do_header("$f->{name} Forum");
print qq(<h2>$f->{name} Forum</h2>\n);
print $f->{desc};
&do_nav;
```

Now we make a few changes. First we'll have MySQL format the message date in a readable format, by adding a date_format to the prepare statement:

```
# fetch the individual messages in the forum, and
# display the info.
$sth = $dbh->prepare("select *,date_format(date, '%c/%e/%Y') as
nicedate from messages where forum=$forum_id and thread_id=0
order by date desc") or &dbdie;
$rv = $sth->execute;
$count = 0;
```

Next we add another select (again using a different database statement handle, $asth, so as not to overwrite the data from the main select statement). As you can see, we're selecting the count of all messages that are follow-ups to the current message being listed. We also want the date the most recent follow-up was posted. Remember to wrap my() around any new variable declarations you make:

```
while ($f = $sth->fetchrow_hashref) {
    my($asth) = $dbh->prepare("select count(*),
date_format(max(date), '%c/%e/%Y') as nicedate from
messages where thread_id=$f->{id}");
    $rv = $asth->execute;
    my($r,$m) = $asth->fetchrow_array;
    my($responses);
    if ($r == 1) {
        $responses = "- 1 response on $m";
    } elsif ($r > 1) {
        $responses = "- $r responses, last on $m";
    } else {
        $responses = "posted on $f->{nicedate}";
    }
```

The only other change is to add the $responses info to the message line:

```
print qq(<b><a href="message.cgi?$f->{id}">
$f->{subject}</a></b>($f->{author}) $responses<br>\n);
```

The rest of the script remains the same.

⊟ Source code: http://www.cgi101.com/advanced/forums/ch9forum.txt
⇨ Working example: http://www.cgi101.com/advanced/forums/ch9forum.cgi?forum=1

Save the file, and reload forum.cgi in your browser. You should see a message listing that looks something like this:

```
test (jd) - 2 responses, last on 5/26/2002
fnords r us (kira) - 1 response on 5/22/2002
fnords r us (kira) posted on 5/15/2002
test msg (jdh) posted on 5/15/2002
test msg (jdh) posted on 5/15/2002
```

You can change the formatting of this page by modifying the print statement inside the while loop; perhaps you'd like to display each message in a table cell. To do so, change the print line:

```
print qq(<b><a href="message.cgi?$f->{id}">
$f->{subject}</a></b>
    ($f->{author}) $responses<br>\n);
```

To something like this:

```
print qq(<tr><td align="LEFT">
    <b><a href="message.cgi?$f->{id}">
$f->{subject}</a></b> ($f->{author})</td>
<td align="RIGHT">$responses</td></tr>\n);
```

Don't forget to add opening and closing <table></table> tags before and after the while loop.

Experiment with the design of your board and see what looks good to you.

Limiting the Number of Topics Per Page

MySQL conveniently has a LIMIT command, which allows you to limit the number of results returned. You can limit to a single number:

```
select * from messages where thread_id=0 limit 50 order by id;
```

This example will return the first 50 messages in the table (messages numbered 0-49, since MySQL, like Perl, starts counting at 0). Alternately, you can specify records in the middle of the results list:

```
select * from messages where thread_id=0 limit 100,50 order by id;
```

This will return 50 messages, starting with the 100th message that matches the select condition. (messages 100-149).

We'll need to modify forum.cgi to handle a second query string variable. Remember that query string variables are separated by an ampersand (&), so the script should accept the forum ID (required), then an optional message ID to start with:

forum.cgi?forum=1	displays the first 50 messages in forum 1
forum.cgi?forum=1&start=50	displays messages 50-99 in forum 1
forum.cgi?forum=1&start=100	displays messages 100-149 in forum 1

This assumes we're setting the number of messages to display per page at 50. You can adjust this to any number. Here's the new code for parsing and untainting the query string:

```
# here we untaint the query string
if ($cgi->param('forum') =~ /^(\d+)$/) {
    $forum_id = $1;
} else {
    &dienice($cgi->param('forum') . " isn't a valid forum
number.");
}
my($start);
#untaint the limit count
if ($cgi->param('start') =~ /^(\d+)$/) {
  $start = $1;
} else {
  $start = 0;
}
# how many msgs to display per page
my($maxcount) = 50;
```

Next we modify the message select to include the limits:

```
# fetch the individual messages in the forum, and display
# the info.
$sth = $dbh->prepare("select *,date_format(date, '%c/%e/%Y') as
nicedate from messages where forum=$forum_id and thread_id=0
order by date desc limit $start, $maxcount") or &dbdie;
```

Finally we need to add some navigation links to get to the previous/next sets of 50. This goes after the end of the `while` loop that displays the actual messages. If the limit was 0 (starting at the beginning of the forum), there is no "previous" link:

```
my($prev);
if ($start > 0) {
    $prev = $start - $maxcount;
    if ($prev < 0) {
    # this shouldn't really happen, but we'll account
    # for it anyway...
        $prev = 0;
    }
    print qq(<p><a
href="forum.cgi?forum=$forum_id&start=$prev">&lt; Previous
$maxcount</a></p>\n);
}
```

Note we subtract $maxcount from the *current* limit ($start) to get the new starting message number.

And, unless we're at the end of the forum, we need a link to the next 50 messages:

```
if ($count == $maxcount) {
    $next = $start + $maxcount;
    print qq(<p><a
href="forum.cgi?forum=$forum_id&start=$next">Next $maxcount
&gt;</a></p>\n);
}
```

Since we're not counting the actual number of messages in the forum beforehand, we can't know for sure if this is the last page of messages. We're just assuming that if the counter ($count) is equal to $maxcount, then there are probably more messages. If you want to be precise, you should query the db for the exact count before displaying the message loop:

```
$sth = $dbh->prepare("select count(*) from posts where forum=?
and thread_id=0") or &dbdie;
```

```
$rv = $sth->execute($forum_id);
my($msgct) = $sth->fetchrow_array;
```

Now you'll know there are more messages if $msgct is greater than $limit + $maxcount.

Here's the entire source code for forum.cgi now, with all of the modifications in place.

```
#!/usr/bin/perl -Tw
use strict;
use lib '.';
use MyBoard;

# declare variables
my($forum_id, $sth, $rv, $f, $count);

# here we untaint the query string
if ($cgi->param('forum') =~ /^(\d+)$/) {
    $forum_id = $1;
} else {
    &dienice($cgi->param('forum') . " isn't a valid forum
number.");
}

my($start);
#untaint the limit count
if ($cgi->param('start') =~ /^(\d+)$/) {
  $start = $1;
} else {
  $start = 0;
}

# how many msgs to display per page
my($maxcount) = 50;

# get the name & info on this forum from the forums table
$sth = $dbh->prepare("select * from forums where id=$forum_id")
or &dbdie;
$rv = $sth->execute;
$f = $sth->fetchrow_hashref;
&do_header("$f->{name} Forum");
print qq(<h2>$f->{name} Forum</h2>\n);
print $f->{desc};
```

```
&do_nav;

# fetch the individual messages in the forum, and
# display the info.
$count = 0;
$sth = $dbh->prepare("select *,date_format(date, '%c/%e/%Y') as
nicedate from messages where forum=$forum_id and thread_id=0
order by date desc limit $start, $maxcount") or &dbdie;
$rv = $sth->execute;
while ($f = $sth->fetchrow_hashref) {
   my($asth) = $dbh->prepare("select count(*),
date_format(max(date), '%c/%e/%Y') as nicedate from
messages where thread_id=$f->{id}");
   $rv = $asth->execute;
   my($r,$m) = $asth->fetchrow_array;
   my($responses);
   if ($r == 1) {
       $responses = "- 1 response on $m";
   } elsif ($r > 1) {
       $responses = "- $r responses, last on $m";
   } else {
       $responses = "posted on $f->{nicedate}";
   }
   print qq(<b><a href="message.cgi?$f->{id}">
$f->{subject}</a></b> ($f->{author}) $responses<br>\n);
   $count = $count + 1;
}

if ($count == 0) {
   print qq(No messages.<p>\n);
} else {
   my($prev);
   if ($start > 0) {
       $prev = $start - $maxcount;
       if ($prev < 0) {
          $prev = 0;
       }
       print qq(<p><a
href="forum.cgi?forum=$forum_id&start=$prev">&lt; Previous
$maxcount</a></p>\n);
   }
   if ($count == $maxcount) {
```

```
        my($next);
        $next = $start + $maxcount;
        print qq(<p><a
href="forum.cgi?forum=$forum_id&start=$next">Next $maxcount
&gt;</a></p>\n);
        }

}

&do_nav;
&do_footer;

sub do_nav {
    print qq(<hr><center>\n);
    print qq(<p><a href="newmsg.cgi?$forum_id">Compose New
Message</a> | );
    print qq(<a href="search.cgi?$forum_id">Search This
Forum</a></p>);
    print qq(</center><hr>\n);
}
```

⊟ Source code: http://www.cgi101.com/advanced/forums/forum.txt
⇨ Working example: http://www.cgi101.com/advanced/forums/forum.cgi

You won't actually be able to test the previous/next links until you have 50 messages posted; for testing purposes you may want to change $maxcount to 5, so you can see the limits in action.

Searching the Forums

A nice feature for a message board system is the ability to search the forums. This is especially useful (and important) if your boards are for technical or customer support. It's fairly easy to make your forums searchable by taking advantage of MySQL's matching capabilities.

MySQL has two mattern matching operators: `LIKE` and `REGEXP` (or `RLIKE`, an alias for `REGEXP`). The `LIKE` operator is very basic and has two wildcard characters used for matching: _ (underscore), which matches any single character, and % (percent), which matches any group of characters. If you want to match any message with the phrase "blue", you would use:

```
select * from messages where message like "%blue%";
```

The wildcard is needed on either side of the search phrase in order to match the phrase anywhere in the message field. The above will match things like "It's a blue moon tonight", "Bluebirds are singing", and "I like blue." If you omit the leading %:

```
select * from messages where message like "blue%";
```

This will only match "Bluebirds are singing" or other messages where "blue" is the first word (or part of the first word). If you omit the wildcards altogether, it's no different than using = (equals):

```
select * from messages where message like "blue";
```

is the same as

```
select * from messages where message = "blue";
```

If you want to match multiple phrases, you have to add another LIKE match:

```
select * from messages where message like "%blue%" and message
like "%red%";
```

MySQL also can do regular expression pattern matching using the REGEXP operator. (Note that REGEXP is specific to MySQL; if you're using some other database server, you should stick with LIKE as it's standard SQL.) The syntax for a regexp query is:

```
select * from messages where message regexp "pattern";
```

You can also use RLIKE in lieu of REGEXP. Patterns can be of the following form:

^	matches the beginning of a string
$	matches the end of a string
.	matches any character (including newlines)
*a**	matches the pattern *a* zero or more times
a+	matches the pattern *a* one or more times
a?	matches the pattern *a* zero or one times
abc|def	matches either pattern "abc" or "def"
a{m,n}	matches the pattern *a* at least *m* times but no more than *n* times
[a-z]	matches any character in the set (in this example, the set is the entire lowercase alphabet)
[ahg]	matches any of the characters in this set (either "a", "h", or "g")

These patterns are identical to the regular expression syntax in Perl 5.

So, if you want to match messages that include either "red" *or* "blue", you would use:

```
select * from messages where message rlike "red|blue";
```

To match messages that include *both* words ("red" *and* "blue"):

```
select * from messages where message rlike 'red' and
message rlike 'blue';
```

Setting up the CGI

First we need a search form; this is mainly just HTML, although we are going to pass the forum ID in to the search script so we can limit the search to a specific forum. Start a new file named search.cgi:

```perl
#!/usr/bin/perl -wT

use strict;
use lib '.';
use MyBoard;

my($forum_id, $sth, $rv, $f);

# untaint the query string
if ($ENV{QUERY_STRING} =~ /^(\d+)$/) {
    $forum_id = $1;
} else {
    &dienice("$ENV{QUERY_STRING} isn't a valid forum
number.");
}

# get the name & info on this forum from the forums table
$sth = $dbh->prepare("select * from forums where id=$forum_id")
or &dbdie;
$rv = $sth->execute;
$f = $sth->fetchrow_hashref;
&do_header("Search the $f->{name} Forum");
print qq(<h2>Search the $f->{name} Forum</h2>\n);

print <<EndHTML;

<form action="search2.cgi" method="POST">
<input type="hidden" name="forum" value="$forum_id">
Search for: <input type="text" name="keywords" size=40>
<input type="submit" value="Search">
</form>
<p>
EndHTML

&do_footer;
```

🖻 Source code: http://www.cgi101.com/advanced/forums/search.txt
⇨ Working example: http://www.cgi101.com/advanced/forums/search.cgi

Next we'll write the script to search for results and display them. How you handle the search can mean the difference between a good search engine and a bad one. In general, the search should find messages that contain *all* of the keywords listed. So a keyword search with the keywords "green tree frog" should do:

```
where message rlike 'green' and message rlike 'tree' and
message rlike 'frog'
```

We'll handle this by splitting the incoming keywords on whitespace.

Start a new file named search2.cgi:

```perl
#!/usr/bin/perl -wT
use strict;
use lib '.';
use MyBoard;

my($forum_id, $keywords, @keyary, @searchary, $searchstr, $sth,
$rv, $count, $f, $i);

$forum_id = $cgi->param('forum');
$keywords = $cgi->param('keywords');

# split keywords on whitespace
@keyary = split(/\s+/, $keywords);

# loop through the keywords - untaint them (only allow
# alphanumeric words)
# then push them into a search array.

foreach $i (@keyary) {
    if ($i =~ /^(\w+)$/) { # it's alphanumeric
        push(@searchary, qq(message RLIKE '$1'));
    } else {
        &dienice("Please use alphanumeric keywords (letters and
numbers only).");
    }
}
# now join the search array so you have a string of the
# format: "message RLIKE 'foo' and message RLIKE 'bar'"

$searchstr = join(" and ", @searchary);

&do_header("Search Results");
```

```
print qq(<h2>Search Results</h2>\n);

$sth = $dbh->prepare("select *, date_format(date, '%c/%e/%Y')
as nicedate from messages where forum=? and $searchstr") or
&dbdie;
$rv = $sth->execute($forum_id);
$count = 0;
while ($f = $sth->fetchrow_hashref) {
    print qq(<b><a
      href="message.cgi?$f->{id}">$f->{subject}</a></b>
      ($f->{author}) posted on $f->{nicedate}<br>\n);
    $count = $count + 1;
}

print qq(<p>$count results.<p>\n);
&do_footer;
```

Source code: http://www.cgi101.com/advanced/forums/search2.txt

Save, "chmod 755", and test your search script.

At this point you've completed all of the CGI scripts that drive the message boards. All that's left are scripts to make administering the boards easier.

11 Setting Up an Admin Area

Many of the board admin functions (such as creating new forums and deleting messages) can be done manually in MySQL. However this is somewhat unwieldy; for example, if you delete a message that has follow-ups, you'll orphan the follow-up messages. You also can't let anyone else administer your board (unless you trust them with your MySQL password). So for convenience, we're going to add a Web-based admin area to let you (or other board admins) perform these functions from your browser.

Create a new directory in your message board directory:

```
mkdir admin
chmod 755 admin
cd admin
```

Password Protection

Now you need to protect the admin area with a password, so that regular users can't get in and make changes to your board. We'll use basic HTTP authentication for this. Create a new file named .htaccess:

```
AuthUserFile /full/path/to/.htpasswd
AuthName "Message Board Administration"
AuthType Basic

require valid-user
```

Save and "chmod 644" this file.

Be sure to change the AuthUserFile path to the current directory. If you aren't sure what

it is, type `pwd` in the shell. If the return result is
`/home/yourname/public_html/forums/admin`, then you want AuthUserFile to be
`/home/yourname/public_html/forums/admin/.htpasswd` .

Now you need to create the password file. You'll need to use the `htpasswd` program to
do this. It is included with the Apache server, usually in the support subdirectory under
the server root (try /usr/local/apache/bin, for Apache 1.3 and later). If you can't find it
or your server doesn't have this program, you can download one or write your own.
There is a htpasswd module on CPAN at http://search.cpan.org/search?dist=Apache-
Htpasswd.

Once you've located the `htpasswd` program, type:

```
htpasswd -c .htpasswd username
```

Change the username in this example to the name you wish to use for your admin
account. You'll be prompted for a password for the new user.

Next you should chmod the newly created .htpasswd file:

```
chmod 644 .htpasswd
```

If you want to add more users to the password file, you don't need the `-c` option:

```
htpasswd newusername
```

`-c` means "create the file", and is only needed the first time.

Keep in mind that unless you run the admin area over https (a secure server), your
password will be transmitted unencrypted, and could be intercepted by hackers.

Admin Index

Now we'll set up the index page for the admin area. This will be a basic page for now;
we'll add pieces to it as we write the back-end code.

Start a new file named index.cgi:

```
#!/usr/bin/perl -wT
use strict;
use lib '../';
use MyBoard;
```

```
&do_header("Board Administration");
print qq(<h2>Board Administration</h2>\n);

# code will go here

print qq(<p><a href="$url/">Back to Forums</a></p>\n);

&do_footer;
```

Source code: http://www.cgi101.com/advanced/forums/adminindex.txt

Save and "chmod 755" the file. The syntax `use lib '../'` indicates to include the directory *above* this one in the search path. If you omit it (or use the wrong path) Perl will raise an error about not being able to find MyBoard.pm.

Now try accessing your admin page - the URL will be the same as your message board URL, with /admin/ tacked onto the end. Be sure it prompts you for the username and password you entered into your .htaccess file.

Once you've verified that the password and index page both work, you're ready to move on to writing the admin scripts.

References

HTTP authentication - http://httpd.apache.org/docs/howto/auth.html
htpasswd man page - http://httpd.apache.org/docs/programs/htpasswd.html

12 Creating, Editing and Deleting Forums

Since the first thing you're likely to want to do with your new board is add new forums, we'll start by writing a script to do that.

Creating Forums

Edit your index.cgi file again and add this code block. This is a basic HTML input form, with spaces for the relevant info for the new forum:

```
print <<EndCreate;
<u>Create Forum:</u><br>
<form action="create.cgi" method="POST">
<table border=0>
<tr>
  <th>Forum Name</th>
  <th>Description</th>
  <th>Rank</th>
  <th>Expire Days*</th>
  <th></th>
</tr>
</tr>
  <tr><td><input type="text" size=25 name="name"></td>
  <td><input type="text" name="desc" size=60></td>
  <td><select name="rank">
<option>1
<option>2
<option>3
<option>4
<option>5
```

```
</select></td>
  <td><input type="text" name="expire" size=3 value="90"></td>
  <td><input type="submit" value="Create"></td>
</tr>
</table>
</form>
<p>*Expire days - the maximum # of days to keep posts. Default
is 90 days.
</p>
<hr>
EndCreate
```

Now you need a script to take the form input, do a little taint checking, and insert the data into the database. Start a new file named create.cgi and enter the following code:

```
#!/usr/bin/perl -wT
use strict;
use lib '../';
use MyBoard;

# the expire time should always be a number, so
# untaint it.

# if it's NOT a number, we won't bother untainting,
# we'll set it to a default of 90 days.

my($expire) = 90;

if ($cgi->param('expire') =~ /^(\d+)$/ and $1 > 0) {
    $expire = $1;
}

# the forum name shouldn't have any HTML tags in it,
# since we're going to use it in the <title> tag of
# each specific forum.  Untaint it by allowing
# only letters, numbers, dashes and spaces.  (If you
# installed the HTML::TagFilter module, you may want
# to use that instead.)

my($name);
if ($cgi->param('name') =~ /^([\w\-\s]+)$/) {
    $name = $1;
} else {
```

```
    &dienice("'" . $cgi->param('name') . "' is not a valid forum
name.");
    }

    my($sth) = $dbh->prepare("insert into forums(name, description,
    rank, expiretime) values (?, ?, ?, ?)");
    $sth->execute($cgi->param('name'), $cgi->param('desc'),
    $cgi->param('rank'), $expire) or &dbdie;

    # redirect back to the admin index page

    print $cgi->redirect("$url/admin/");
```

⊟ Source code: http://www.cgi101.com/advanced/forums/admincreate.txt

Save and "chmod 755" the file. Since the forums table auto-increments the forum ID, we don't need to specify a forum ID when inserting the data. MySQL will do the right thing and assign the next highest number as the new forum's ID.

Test out your script by creating a new forum.

Editing Forums

Next we're going to add scripts to edit the forum name, description, rank and/or expire time. Edit your index.cgi again and add this after the "Create Forum" block:

```
    # Edit/Delete Forums
    #
    print qq(
    <u>Edit Forums:</u>
    <p>
    <table border=0>
    <tr>
        <th align="LEFT">Forum Name</th>
        <th align="LEFT">Description</th>
        <th>Rank</th>
        <th># of Posts</th>
        <th>Expire Days</th>
        <th></th>
        <th></th>
```

```
</tr>
);

my($sth) = $dbh->prepare("select forums.*, count(messages.id)
as msgcount from forums left join messages on forums.id =
messages.forum group by forums.id order by rank, name") or
&dbdie;
my($rv) = $sth->execute;
my($f);
while ($f = $sth->fetchrow_hashref) {
    print qq(
<tr>
    <td> <a href="../forum.cgi?forum=$f->{id}">
$f->{name}</a> </td>
    <td> $f->{description} </td>
    <td align="CENTER"> $f->{rank} </td>
    <td align="CENTER"> $f->{msgcount} </td>
    <td align="CENTER"> $f->{expiretime} </td>
    <td> <a href="edit.cgi?$f->{id}">[edit]</a> </td>
    <td> <a href="delete.cgi?$f->{id}">[delete]</a> </td>
</tr>
    );
}
print qq(</table>\n <hr>\n);
```

Source code: http://www.cgi101.com/advanced/forums/adminindex2.txt

Save it, then reload the page in your browser. You should see a list of all the forums in your database, including the one(s) you just added when you tested the create script.

Notice here we've using the same LEFT JOIN query as in the index.cgi from Chapter 4, so we can display the message count for each forum. We're also formatting the data with a table so that it's easy to read in the browser.

Next we need to create edit.cgi, which displays the forum data inside a table like the one we used for "create forum".

```
#!/usr/bin/perl -wT
use strict;
use lib '../';
use MyBoard;
```

```perl
&dohdr("Edit Forum");

my($forum, $i, $f);

if ($ENV{QUERY_STRING} !~ /^(\d+)$/) {
    &dienice("$ENV{QUERY_STRING} isn't a valid forum number.");
} else {
    $forum = $1;
}

my($sth) = $dbh->prepare("select * from forums where id=?");
my($rv) = $sth->execute($forum);
$f = $sth->fetchrow_hashref;

# in case someone put quotes in these, escape them
# so they don't break the form

$f->{name} =~ s/\"/\&quot;/g;
$f->{description} =~ s/\"/\&quot;/g;

my($ranks) = "";
foreach $i (1..5) {
    if ($f->{rank} == $i) {
        $ranks .= "<option selected>$i\n";
    } else {
        $ranks .= "<option>$i\n";
    }
}

print <<EndHTML;
<form action="edit2.cgi" method="POST">
<input type="hidden" name="forum" value="$forum">
<table border=0>
<tr>
  <th>Forum Name</th>
  <th>Description</th>
  <th>Rank</th>
  <th>Expire Days*</th>
  <th></th>
</tr>
<tr>
  <td><input type="text" size=25 name="name"
```

```
            value="$f->{name}"></td>
     <td><input type="text" name="desc" size=60
         value="$f->{description}"></td>
     <td><select name="rank">
  $ranks
  </select></td>
     <td><input type="text" name="expire" size=3
         value="$f->{expiretime}"></td>
     <td><input type="submit" value="Save Changes"></td>
  </tr>
  </table><p>
  *Expire days - the maximum number of days to keep posts.
  Default 90.


  EndHTML


  &do_footer;
```

⊟ Source code: http://www.cgi101.com/advanced/forums/adminedit.txt

Save and "chmod 755" the file, then click the "Edit" link next to one of the forum names in your admin index page to be sure it loads properly.

Now we need edit2.cgi, which is so much like create.cgi that the easiest thing to do is to copy that file and make a few changes:

```
     cp create.cgi edit2.cgi
     chmod 755 edit2.cgi
```

Then edit the edit2.cgi script and change the SQL statements to:

```
     my($sth) = $dbh->prepare("replace into forums(id, name,
     description, rank, expiretime) values (?, ?, ?, ?, ?)");
     $sth->execute($cgi->param('forum'), $cgi->param('name'),
     $cgi->param('desc'), $cgi->param('rank'), $expire) or &dbdie;
```

The replace into syntax replaces the data for a given record if it already exists in the table; if it doesn't exist (which shouldn't happen in this case), replace into will create the record.

To save on code, you could modify create.cgi to handle both creating and editing forums. You'd need to add another hidden parameter to your form input fields to indicate which action the script should take.

Deleting Forums

Next we need to handle deleting forums. This should also delete all messages in those forums. To avoid accidents, we're going to make the first step of the delete process an "are you SURE?" page. Start a new file named delete.cgi and enter the following:

```perl
#!/usr/bin/perl -wT
use strict;
use lib '../';
use MyBoard;

&do_header("Delete Forum");
my($forum);
if ($ENV{QUERY_STRING} !~ /^(\d+)$/) {
    &dienice("$ENV{QUERY_STRING} isn't a valid forum number.");
} else {
    $forum = $1;
}

my($sth) = $dbh->prepare("select * from forums where id=?") or
&dbdie;
my($rv) = $sth->execute($forum) or &dbdie;
if ($rv < 1) {
    &dienice("Forum $forum doesn't exist.");
}
my($f);
$f = $sth->fetchrow_hashref;

$sth = $dbh->prepare("select count(*) from messages where
forum=?") or &dbdie;
$rv = $sth->execute($forum) or &dbdie;
my($msgct) = $sth->fetchrow_array;

print <<EndHTML;
<h2>Are You Sure?</h2>
<p>
Deleting forum \#$forum - $f->{name}
</p>
<form action="delete2.cgi" method="POST">
```

```
<input type="hidden" name="forum" value="$forum">
<p>
This forum contains $msgct messages. Do you really want to
delete it?
<input type="submit" value="Yes">
</form></p>
<p>
Or <b><a href="index.cgi">Return to Administration</a></b> if
you don't want to delete this forum.
</p>
EndHTML

&do_footer;
```

🖥 Source code: http://www.cgi101.com/advanced/forums/admindelete.txt

Save and "chmod 755" the file, then click one of the "Delete" links on the admin index page.

And finally we create delete2.cgi:

```
#!/usr/bin/perl -wT
use strict;
use lib '../';
use MyBoard;

&do_header("Delete Forum");

if ($cgi->param('forum') !~ /^(\d+)$/) {
    &dienice($cgi->param('forum') . " isn't a valid forum
number.");
} else {
    $forum = $1;
}

my($sth) = $dbh->prepare("select * from forums where id=?") or
&dbdie;
my($rv) = $sth->execute($forum) or &dbdie;
if ($rv < 1) {
    &dienice("Forum $forum doesn't exist.");
}
my($f);
$f = $sth->fetchrow_hashref;
```

```
$dbh->do("delete from forums where id=$forum") or &dbdie;
$dbh->do("delete from messages where forum=$forum") or &dbdie;

print <<EndHTML;
<h2>Deleted</h2>
<p>
Forum \#$forum - $f->{name} Deleted.
</p>

<p>
<b><a href="index.cgi">Return to Administration</a></b>
</p>
EndHTML

&do_footer;
```

Source code: http://www.cgi101.com/advanced/forums/admindelete2.txt

Save, "chmod 755", and test it out by deleting one of the test forums you created earlier.

Deleting and Expiring Messages

Deleting individual messages is a little more complex than deleting entire forums. Because of the way we built our earlier scripts, if we end up deleting a message that is the original post in a thread, then we'll orphan the rest of the thread. To counter this problem we'll add a `delete` subroutine to the MyBoard module.

Delete Subroutine

This subroutine accepts the ID of a message to be deleted, deletes it from the database, then searches out follow-ups. If a follow-up is found, the first follow-up is reset to an original message (by changing its `thread_id` to 0), and the rest of the thread is set so that the `thread_id` is the ID of the new original message in the thread.

Edit MyBoard.pm and add the new `delete` subroutine at the bottom (but before the `1;` at the very end):

```
sub delete {
    my($msgid) = @_;
    my($sth, $rv, $f);
    $sth = $dbh->prepare("delete from messages where
            id=?") or &dbdie;
    $rv = $sth->execute($msgid);
    $sth = $dbh->prepare("select * from messages where
            thread_id=? limit 1") or &dbdie;
    $rv = $sth->execute($msgid);
    if ($f = $sth->fetchrow_hashref) {
        $dbh->do("update messages set thread_id=0 where
                id=$f->{id}") or &dbdie;
        $dbh->do("update messages set thread_id=$f->{id}
                where thread_id=$msgid") or &dbdie;
```

```
        }
    }
```

Be sure to also add the `delete` subroutine to the export list at the top of MyBoard.pm. Since `delete` isn't a function that will be used by most scripts, we're going to put it into the `EXPORT_OK` array rather than `EXPORT`:

```
@EXPORT = qw(dienice do_header do_footer dbdie $dbh $cgi);
@EXPORT_OK = qw(delete);
```

This means any script wanting to use the `delete` function will have to specifically include it. So for example, if you have a script that needs to use `delete`, as well as all of the functions in `@EXPORT`, you must use:

```
use MyBoard qw(:DEFAULT delete);
```

`:DEFAULT` means to include everything in the module's `@EXPORT` list.

Save MyBoard.pm. Be sure to test your changes by reloading one of the forum's scripts in your browser! If you introduce errors into your module, you'll break the entire message board, so it's best to check for them immediately.

Now edit index.cgi in the admin directory and add the following form block. Since you're probably going to delete messages more often than you create new forums, it's best to put this above the create/edit/delete forums sections:

```
# Cancel Messages
print <<EndCancel;
<form action="cancel.cgi" method="POST">
<u>Cancel Message</u> #:<input type="text" name="msgid" size=5>
<input type="submit" value="Cancel Message">
<font size=-1>You will be able to view the message, and the IP
address it was posted from, before canceling it.</font>
</form>
<hr>
EndCancel
```

Now we want cancel.cgi to display the message being canceled, plus the header info of any follow-up messages. Then it should provide us with a button to cancel either the offending message or the entire thread.

To save some typing, it's easiest to copy message.cgi from the main directory into the admin directory and make changes to that:

```
cp ../message.cgi cancel.cgi
chmod 755 cancel.cgi
```

Now you can make changes where needed in cancel.cgi. Comment tags will show you where changes have been made:

```perl
#!/usr/bin/perl -Tw
use strict;
# correct the directory for use lib
use lib '../';
use MyBoard;

my($msgid, $sth, $rv, $msg, $resp);

# untaint the message number
# this is different from message.cgi in that it's a
# posted value rather than the query string.
if ($cgi->param('msgid') =~ /^(\d+)$/) {
    $msgid = $1;
} else {
    &dienice($cgi->param('msgid') . " isn't a valid message
number.");
}

$sth = $dbh->prepare("select messages.*,
date_format(date,'%c/%e/%Y %r') as
nicedate, forums.name from messages, forums where
messages.forum = forums.id and (messages.id=? or thread_id=?)
order by thread_id, date") or &dbdie;
$rv = $sth->execute($msgid, $msgid);
if ($rv < 1) {
    &dienice("Message ID $msgid doesn't exist.");
}
$msg = $sth->fetchrow_hashref;

# Change the page title
&do_header("Delete Message #$msgid: $msg->{subject}");
print qq(<h2>Delete Message</h2>\n);

&showpost($msg);

# add message-only cancel button
```

```perl
# the hidden field "action" tells cancel2.cgi to
# cancel the one message.
print qq(<form action="cancel2.cgi" method="POST">
<input type="hidden" name="msgid" value="$msgid">
<input type="hidden" name="action" value="message">
<input type="submit" value="Cancel Message">
</form>);

print qq(<hr>\n);

if ($msg->{thread_id} == 0) {
    $resp = 0;
    while ($msg = $sth->fetchrow_hashref) {
        if ($resp == 0) {
            print "<b>Responses:</b><br>\n";
            $resp = 1;
        }
        # don't show the full text of followups -
        # just the subject line,
        # author, and date posted.
        print qq(#$msg->{id}: <a
href="../message.cgi?$msg->{id}">$msg->{subject}</a> - posted by
$msg->{author} on $msg->{nicedate}<br>\n);
    }
    # if there aren't any responses, say so:
    if ($resp == 0) {
        print qq(<p>No responses to this message.</p>\n);
    } else {
    # print the cancel-thread button
        print qq(<form action="cancel2.cgi" method="POST">
<input type="hidden" name="msgid" value="$msgid">
<input type="hidden" name="action" value="thread">
<input type="submit" value="Cancel Entire Thread">
</form>);
    }
}

&do_footer;

sub showpost {
    my($hdr);
    my($msg) = @_;
```

```
        $msg->{message} =~ s/\n/<br>\n/g;

        # modify the post to display the author's e-mail
        # and IP addresses as well as the forum name
        print <<EndHTML;
<hr>
<blockquote>
Forum: $msg->{name}<br>
Message #$msg->{id}<br>
Subject: <b>$msg->{subject}</b><br>
Author: $msg->{author} ($msg->{email}) ($msg->{ip})<br>
Posted: $msg->{nicedate}<br>
<p>
$msg->{message}
</p>
</blockquote>
EndHTML
        }
```

⊟ Source code: http://www.cgi101.com/advanced/forums/admincancel.txt

The script may look lengthy, but we've actually changed very little from the original message.cgi script.

Now we need the cancel2.cgi script to do the actual work. Here we're going to import the delete function we wrote earlier in MyBoard.pm, but we'll only be using it if we're canceling an individual message (and not an entire thread). Since the delete subroutine changes the thread_id of the rest of the thread, it's easier to use a simple DBI do query to delete entire threads.

Start a new file named cancel2.cgi and enter the following:

```
#!/usr/bin/perl -Tw
use strict;
use lib '../';
use MyBoard qw(:DEFAULT delete);

my($msgid, $sth, $rv, $msg, $resp);

# untaint the message number
```

```
if ($cgi->param('msgid') =~ /^(\d+)$/) {
    $msgid = $1;
} else {
    &dienice($cgi->param('msgid') . " isn't a valid message
number.");
}

&do_header("Delete Message - Results");

print qq(<h2>Delete Message - Results</h2>\n);

if ($cgi->param('action') eq "thread") {
# be sure to enclose the OR in parentheses here -
# (id=$msgid OR thread_id=$msgid)
   $dbh->do("delete from messages where
      (id=$msgid or thread_id=$msgid)");
   print qq(<p>Thread deleted.</p>\n);
} else {
   &delete($msgid);
   print qq(<p>Message #$msgid deleted.</p>\n);
}

print qq(<p><b><a href="index.cgi">Back to
Administration</a></b></p>\n);

&do_footer;
```

⊟ Source code: http://www.cgi101.com/advanced/forums/admincancel2.txt

Save and "chmod 755" the file, then try canceling an individual message with no follow-ups, then an entire message thread.

Expiring Old Messages

When we created the forums table we added an expiretime column representing the number of days to keep messages in each forum. We'll need a script now to expire old messages. This script is not a CGI, but instead will run on a schedule (such as once every night) from your crontab.

Once again we'll have MySQL do most of the work here. The MySQL date_sub function allows you to subtract a specified time interval from a date column in your table. (There is also a corresponding date_add function for adding dates.) The syntax is DATE_SUB(date, INTERVAL expr type). date can be a column name, a string or a MySQL function of type DATE or DATETIME. expr is usually a number, and type can be a number of different time values such as SECOND, MINUTE, HOUR, DAY, MONTH, YEAR, and several others (consult the MySQL manual at http://www.mysql.com/ for a complete list and further examples). We'll be using date_sub to select the messages in each forum that were posted more than expiretime days ago, so the actual query is:

```
select id from messages where forum=? and
date < date_sub(current_time(),INTERVAL ? DAY)
```

The forum ID will be passed in as the first parameter, and the forum's expiretime is the second parameter.

Start a new file named expire.pl. You'll need to change the use lib line to the full path to where your MyBoard.pm module is stored (because cron uses different paths than your CGI scripts and will not know where to look).

```
#!/usr/bin/perl -wT
use strict;
use lib '/home/yourname/public_html/cgi-bin/forums';
use MyBoard qw($dbh delete);

my($sth, $rv, $asth, @ary, $f, $g);

$sth = $dbh->prepare("select * from forums where
expiretime > 0");
$rv = $sth->execute;
while ($f = $sth->fetchrow_hashref){
    $asth = $dbh->prepare("select id from messages where
forum=? and date < date_sub(current_time(),INTERVAL ? DAY)");
    $rv = $asth->execute($f->{id},$f->{expiretime});
    @ary = $asth->fetchrow_array;
    foreach $g (@ary) {
        &delete($g);
    }
}
```

🖻 Source code: http://www.cgi101.com/advanced/forums/adminexpire.txt

Save and "chmod 700" this script. (It doesn't need to be mode 755 because it isn't a CGI script.)

You can run the expire manually by typing:

```
./expire.pl
```

in the Unix shell. To schedule it as a `cron` task, edit your crontab by typing
`crontab -e` in the shell. Add a line like so:

```
0 2 * * * /path/to/expire.pl
```

This schedules expire.pl to run at 2am (local machine time) every night. Be sure to
change the path to the actual directory where expire.pl is located (you can type `pwd` in
the shell to find out). Be sure to save your crontab and quit out of the editor.

See "Scheduling Scripts with `cron`" in Chapter 20 of *CGI Programming 101* for more
examples of crontabs.

References

MySQL `DATE_ADD` and `DATE_SUB` functions -
http://www.mysql.com/doc/en/Date_and_time_functions.html#IDX1288

14 Board Administration and Security

One final task to do before launching your new board is to remove the line

```
use CGI::Carp qw(warningsToBrowser fatalsToBrowser);
```

from your MyBoard.pm module. The Carp module is useful for debugging during development, but can also give away too much information to potential hackers. It's best to remove it (or comment it out) after you're done developing.

Once you launch your new board, you (or the board's appointed admins) will always have to keep an eye on it, especially if it's a public message board. Inevitably someone will post spam, foul messages, or repetitive attacks on your board. The intermittent spam can be deleted on a per-message basis using the admin interface. You can also try checking for abusive posts by adding code to postmsg.cgi that will scan the subject, author string and message body for foul language.

If you have spam or abusive messages being posted from the same IP address or range of IP's, you could ban them from your board entirely by using an .htaccess file in the board's main directory:

```
<Limit GET POST>
    order allow,deny
    allow from all
    deny from 192.198.2 .foo.org
    deny from 203.51.
</Limit>
```

Note that there's no space between allow,deny on the order line. Be sure to chmod 644 the .htaccess file so the Webserver can read it.

Banning by IP isn't a sure-fire way of keeping people out, however. IP addresses change often (for dialup users), can be spoofed (by hackers), or can be shared among several users (via proxy servers and firewalls).

Another way to cut down on spam is to require users to register (and get their own username/password) before they can post to the boards. This decreases the usability of your site somewhat, since most people already have dozens of Website usernames and passwords to keep track of, and don't really need one more. But if you're running a members-only or subscription site, you're going to have to have user registration anyway.

There are various ways to implement password protection, whether it's through a flat .htaccess/.htpassword file, a MySQL database, cookies, or a custom Apache module. Visit http://www.cgi101.com/class/password/ for some examples of these.

If you do implement user registration, you may want to modify your messages table to add a username column, so you can keep track of who posted what. (You'll also need to change postmsg.cgi to record their username when they post a message.) Then if one of your users posts spam, you can remove their account (in addition to deleting the offending messages).

You should read through the WWW Security FAQ at http://www.w3.org/Security/Faq/, and specifically the section on "Protecting Confidential Documents at Your Site" (http://www.w3.org/Security/Faq/wwwsf5.html). These issues affect not only your message board but also your entire Website. Code defensively.

Making Backups

Ideally your ISP or Web hosting company will make backups of your data on a regular basis. But you may want to keep your own backup copies just to be safe, or you may want to move your scripts and databases to a new server.

To dump out the entire contents of your MySQL database, including the "create table" definitions, use the `mysqldump` command:

```
mysqldump -u username -p databasename > filename.sql
```

This causes the entire database (with "create table" and "insert" commands for each table and record) to be written to `filename.sql`.

If you only want to dump out the data (without the "create table" definitions), add the `-t` flag to the `mysqldump` statement:

```
mysqldump -t -u username -p databasename > filename.sql
```

To reload the data stored in `filename.sql`, you can redirect the file as input to the `mysql` command:

```
mysql -u username -p dbname < filename.sql
```

You will probably only want to do this over a blank database.

Type `mysqldump` or `mysql -h` in the Unix shell for more help and examples of these commands.

References

`mysqldump` - http://www.mysql.com/doc/en/mysqldump.html

Conclusion

Now you have your own message board system, in fewer than 1000 lines of code. Hopefully working through this project has given you a feel for how to develop a large CGI application.

You can modify and expand on the design to suit your own site. Here are a few ideas for advanced features you may want to add:

- Password-protect the entire message board area, requiring that only registered users can read and post (or alternately, you could require a password only for posting/replying, thereby allowing casual browsers to read the boards without needing to register)
- Allow users to subscribe via e-mail to a particular message thread (or an entire forum), making the forum a kind of pseudo-mailing list.
- Create a mail alias and procmailrc filter allowing subscribers to post to the forums by e-mailing to that address - making the forums a real mailing list with a Web interface
- Create custom formatting for messages and forums by adding icons, allowing users to have their own avatar icons, emoticons, etc.

You can even use much of the same code to create a Web Log ("blog") or daily news site. See Appendix B for an example.

Online Resources

CGI101.COM (http://www.cgi101.com/) is the official website for this book. Source code for all of the CGI programs in the book are provided. CGI101.com also offers Unix shell accounts and CGI-friendly Web hosting.

Perl.com (http://www.perl.com/) is the official site for Perl on the Web.

The Perl Journal (http://tpj.com/) is an e-zine devoted to the Perl language.

The CGI Resource Index (http://www.cgi-resources.com/) includes links to hundreds of CGI-related sites, including links to programs and scripts, documentation, books, magazine articles, and job listings.

The CGI Programming MetaFAQ (http://www.perl.org/CGI_MetaFAQ.html) has links to numerous other FAQs and useful CGI-related information.

The WWW Security FAQ (http://www.w3.org/Security/Faq/www-security-faq.html) contains more generalized information about security of information on the Web. It has a section on CGI, as well as info on running a secure server, protecting confidential data, safe scripting in Perl, and more.

CGI/Perl Taint Mode FAQ (http://gunther.web66.com/FAQS/taintmode.html) has information about taintperl and secure scripting.

Randal Schwartz writes Perl programming columns for several magazines. The articles are archived on his website at http://www.stonehenge.com/merlyn/columns.html.

There are several Usenet newsgroups for discussing Perl and CGI topics; comp.infosystems.www.authoring.cgi and comp.lang.perl.misc are the two main groups. Read them through your local ISP or using Google Groups (http://groups.google.com/).

PerlMonks (http://www.perlmonks.org/) is a discussion forum for Perl programmers.

The MySQL Website (http://www.mysql.com/) has downloadable software, searchable online documentation, and links to third-party applications.

Converting Your Message Board into a Blog

Web Logs (or "blogs") are all the rage on the Web today. Blogs can be used on personal sites (as an online journal/diary) or on business sites (for daily news). This section will show you how to create your own blog using much of the same code from your message boards.

Anatomy of a Blog

A blog typically consists of one or more daily entries, each of which shows the date the message was posted, an optional title, the message itself, the author's tagline, and a link to comments. Blogs also typically allow for more than one message to be posted per day, which are grouped together under the main date heading.

The comments link takes the reader to a new page that displays the original message, plus all comments people have posted. There's also generally a form (or a link to a form) where readers can post new comments.

The main page also typically includes links to the most recent posts, as well as to archives of previous months.

Comparing Blogs and Forums

A blog doesn't have separate forums, so we won't have a forums table in our SQL database. We will have a messages table, but it won't have a forum ID column.

The main blog page is similar to our forum.cgi page, in that it shows a certain number of messages. But the blog will also show the actual messages themselves, rather than just the message subjects.

The comments link takes the reader to our message.cgi page, which is pretty much the same as the one from the forums.

Only the owner of the blog can post new messages. However, anyone can post follow-up comments (unless you disable that feature).

Setting Up a New MySQL Database

You'll need to create a new MySQL database for your blog. In the shell, use these commands to create the database and get into MySQL:

```
mysqladmin -p create cgiblog

mysql -p mysql
```

Now in MySQL, these commands add the new user and set the database privileges. (Be sure to change the password to something else.)

```
insert into user (Host, User, Password) values ("localhost",
"bloguser", password("fnord"));

insert into db values ("localhost", "cgiblog", "bloguser", "Y",
"Y", "Y", "Y", "Y", "Y", "Y", "Y", "Y", "Y");

flush privileges;
```

Now you need to create the messages table. This is identical to the `create` syntax from Chapter 2 except we've omitted the forum column:

```
create table messages(
     id int not null primary key auto_increment,
     author char(255) not null,
     subject char(255) not null,
     email char(255) not null,
     date datetime not null,
     ip char(255) not null,
     message text not null,
     thread_id int not null);
```

If you plan to allow your blog to be searchable, you'll also want to add the indexes:

```
create index threadid_index on messages(thread_id);
create fulltext index msg_index on messages (message);
```

Once you've created the table, quit out of MySQL.

Blog Scripts

Create a new blog directory:

```
mkdir blog
chmod 755 blog
```

We'll be reusing the MyBoard.pm module, so copy MyBoard.pm from your forums directory into the new blog directory. Edit MyBoard.pm and change the $dbh line to use the new database name and password:

```
our $dbh = DBI->connect("dbi:mysql:cgiblog", "bloguser",
"fnord", { RaiseError => 1, AutoCommit => 1 }) or
&dienice("Can't connect to database: $DBI::errstr");
```

Also change the base $url (use your URL and not cgi101's!):

```
our $url = "http://www.cgi101.com/advanced/blog";
```

And if you commented out or deleted the CGI::Carp line, be sure to re-add it:

```
use CGI::Carp qw(warningsToBrowser fatalsToBrowser);
```

We're going to add a new global variable for the blog title (change this to your own title):

```
our $btitle = "Test Blog";
```

Most blogs include a tagline that shows the author's name linked to an e-mail or Web address. Since this is used in several places in our blog code (in index.cgi as well as message.cgi), we'll add a subroutine in the MyBoard.pm module to turn e-mail addresses or web URLs into HTML links. You could download a Perl module to do this, but for now we'll just write a subroutine to do it. This subroutine matches on a regexp pattern (see the "Regular Expressions" chapter in *CGI Programming 101* for more examples of regexps).

The subroutine will be called like so:

```
&linkify("author name", "www.fnordly.com");
```

The result of the above should be a string like this:

```
<a href="http://www.fnordly.com">author name</a>
```

If the link passed to linkify is not a valid URL or e-mail address, the subroutine doesn't build a link at all, and just returns the original string.

```
sub linkify {
    my($str, $link) = @_;
    if ($link =~ /[\w\-]+\@[\w\-]+\.[\w\-]+/) {
        return qq(<a href="mailto:$link">$str</a>);
    } elsif ($link =~
        /^(http:\/\/)*([\w\-\.\/]+\.[\w\-]+)/ ) {
        return qq(<a href="http://$2">$str</a>);
    } else {
        return $str;
    }
}
```

You can also add an optional subroutine to translate emoticons such as :) :(and ;) into images:

```
sub smiliefy {
    my($str) = @_;
    my($smile) = qq(<img src="img/smile.gif"
        width="18" height="18">);
    my($frown) = qq(<img src="img/frown.gif"
        width="18" height="18">);
    my($wink) = qq(<img src="img/wink.gif"
        width="18" height="18">);
    # remember that ()'s have to be escaped with
    # a backslash in regexps
    $str =~ s/:\)/$smile/g;
    $str =~ s/:\(/$frown/g;
    $str =~ s/;\)/$wink/g;
    return $str;
}
```

Then later in your blog code you can translate the emoticons by passing the message body to the smiliefy subroutine:

```
print &smiliefy($message);
```

Don't forget to add $btitle, linkify and smiliefy to the EXPORT line:

```
@EXPORT = qw(dienice do_header do_footer dbdie $dbh $cgi $url
$btitle linkify smiliefy);
```

Save the file.

Source code: http://www.cgi101.com/advanced/blog/MyBoard.txt

index.cgi

The blog's index.cgi is very similar to the forum.cgi script from the message boards. You can either copy that script and make changes, or write index.cgi from scratch. The main difference here is that we'll be displaying the actual message text for each original message (rather than just the message subjects), and we'll also be changing $maxcount to a smaller number (since 50 messages would be a bit overwhelming on one page).

```perl
#!/usr/bin/perl -Tw
use strict;
use lib '.';
use MyBoard;

# declare variables
my($sth, $rv, $f, $count);

my($limit);
# untaint the limit count
if ($cgi->param('start') =~ /^(\d+)$/) {
  $limit = $1;
} else {
  $limit = 0;
}

# how many msgs to display per page
my($maxcount) = 5;

&do_header($btitle);
print qq(<h2>$btitle</h2>\n);

# this will be used for grouping messages by day
my($today) = "";
```

```perl
$count = 0;

# delete the forum_id stuff in the query,
# alter the date format to "Thursday, May 8, 2002"
# and format the time to "12:30 PM"
#
$sth = $dbh->prepare("select *,date_format(date, '%W, %M %e,
%Y') as nicedate, date_format(date, '%l:%i %p') as nicetime
from messages where thread_id=0 order by date desc limit
$limit, $maxcount") or &dbdie;

$rv = $sth->execute;
while ($f = $sth->fetchrow_hashref) {
    my($asth) = $dbh->prepare("select count(*) from messages
where thread_id=$f->{id}");
    $rv = $asth->execute;
    my($r) = $asth->fetchrow_array;
    my($responses);
    if ($r == 1) {
        $responses = "1 comment";
    } elsif ($r > 1) {
        $responses = "$r comments";
    } else {
        $responses = "0 comments";
    }
    # print the date, if we haven't already...
    if ($f->{nicedate} ne $today) {
        if ($today ne "") {
            print qq(<hr>\n);
        }
        print qq(<h3>$f->{nicedate}</h3>\n);
        $today = $f->{nicedate};
    }
    print qq(<b>$f->{subject}</b><p>\n);
    # smiliefy is optional...
    print &smiliefy($f->{message}), qq(<p>\n);
    my($author) = &linkify($f->{author}, $f->{email});
    print qq(<font size="-1"><a
href="message.cgi?$f->{id}">#$f->{id}</a> | Posted by $author
at $f->{nicetime} | <a
href="message.cgi?$f->{id}">$responses</a></font><p>\n);
```

```
        $count = $count + 1;
    }

    if ($count == 0) {
        print qq(No messages.<p>\n);
    } else {
        my($prev);
        if ($limit > 0) {
            $prev = $limit - $maxcount;
            if ($prev < 0) {
                $prev = 0;
            }
            print qq(<p><a href="index.cgi?start=$prev">&lt;
Previous $maxcount</a></p>\n);
        }
        if ($count == $maxcount) {
            my($next);
            $next = $limit + $maxcount;
            print qq(<p><a href="index.cgi?start=$next">Next
$maxcount &gt;</a></p>\n);
        }
    }
    &do_footer;
```

⊟ Source code: http://www.cgi101.com/advanced/blog/index.txt
⇨ Working example: http://www.cgi101.com/advanced/blog/index.cgi

message.cgi

message.cgi is nearly identical to the forums script of the same name, so again, you could either copy this script from your message board, or write it new. We're changing the formatting of the individual messages a little. Also, blog readers can only post follow-ups to the initial message, not to any subsequent comments (although you could add that functionality back if you prefer):

```
#!/usr/bin/perl -Tw
use strict;
use lib '.';
use MyBoard;

my ($msgid, $sth, $rv, $count, $msg, $resp);
```

```
# untaint the query string
if ($ENV{QUERY_STRING} =~ /^(\d+)$/) {
    $msgid = $1;
} else {
    &dienice("$ENV{QUERY_STRING} isn't a valid message
number.");
}

# as with index.cgi, format the date and time nicely
$sth = $dbh->prepare("select *, date_format(date, '%W, %M %e,
%Y') as nicedate, date_format(date, '%l:%i %p') as nicetime
from messages where (messages.id=? or thread_id=?) order by
thread_id, date") or &dbdie;
$rv = $sth->execute($msgid, $msgid);
if ($rv < 1) {
    &dienice("Message $msgid does not exist.");
}
$msg = $sth->fetchrow_hashref;

# if the FIRST message is a follow-up, redirect them to
# the entire page for that message thread.
if ($msg->{thread_id} != 0) {
    print $cgi->redirect(
"$url/message.cgi?$msg->{thread_id}#$msg->{id}");
    exit;
}

&do_header("$btitle: $msg->{nicedate}: $msg->{subject}");
print qq(<h2><a href="$url">$btitle:</a> $msg->{nicedate}:
$msg->{subject}</h2>\n);

&showpost($msg);
$resp = 0;
while ($msg = $sth->fetchrow_hashref) {
    if ($resp == 0) {
        print qq(<h3 align="CENTER">Comments</h3>\n);
        $resp = 1;
    }
    &showpost($msg);
}
```

```
&do_footer;

sub showpost {
    my($hdr);
    my($msg) = @_;

    # smiliefy is optional...
    print &smiliefy($msg->{message}), qq(<p>\n);
    my($author) = &linkify($msg->{author}, $msg->{email});
    print qq(<font size="-1"><a name="$msg->{id}">Msg
#$msg->{id}</a> | Posted by $author on $msg->{nicedate}
$msg->{nicetime}</font><p>\n);

    # only allow follow-ups to the original message
    if ($msg->{thread_id} == 0) {
        print qq(<font size=-1><a
href="reply.cgi?$msg->{id}">Post a Comment</a></font>
<p>\n);
    }
    print qq(<hr noshade>\n);
}
```

🗗 Source code: http://www.cgi101.com/advanced/blog/message.txt
🗢 Working example: http://www.cgi101.com/advanced/blog/message.cgi?1

reply.cgi

In reply.cgi, we've removed the "E-mail Reply" option for follow-ups, as well as the "Do not use HTML tags" line - we're actually going to allow people to use certain HTML tags in their follow-ups:

```
#!/usr/bin/perl -Tw
use strict;
use lib '.';
use MyBoard;

# declare variables
my($msgid, $sth, $rv, $msg, $i, $subject);

# untaint the query string
if ($ENV{QUERY_STRING} =~ /^(\d+)$/) {
```

```
    $msgid = $1;
} else {
    &dienice("$ENV{QUERY_STRING} isn't a valid message
number.");
}

# get the message data
$sth = $dbh->prepare("select * from messages where id=?") or
&dbdie;
$rv = $sth->execute($msgid);
$msg = $sth->fetchrow_hashref;

$subject = $msg->{'subject'};

&do_header("Reply to Message #$msgid: $subject");
print qq(<h2>Reply to Message #$msgid: $subject</h2>\n);

$subject =~ s/\"/&quot;/g;

print <<EndForm;
<form action="postmsg.cgi" method="POST">
<input type="hidden" name="replyto_id" value="$msgid">
<pre>
Your Name: <input type="text" name="name" size=40>
E-mail or Web Address: <input type="text" name="email" size=40>
Subject: <input type="text" name="subject" size=40 value="Re:
$subject">
</pre>

Enter your message below.<p>
<textarea name="message" rows=10 cols=78 wrap="HARD">
</textarea>
<p>
<input type="submit" value="Post Comment">
<input type="reset" value="Erase">
</form>

EndForm

&do_footer;
```

⊟ Source code: http://www.cgi101.com/advanced/blog/reply.txt
⇨ Working example: http://www.cgi101.com/advanced/blog/reply.cgi?1

postmsg.cgi

postmsg.cgi has been changed to have two separate TagFilters. One ($tf) allows a limited set of HTML tags (paragraphs, breaks, italics, bolds, and a href= links), and the other ($tf2) removes *all* tags. We've also omitted the more stringent e-mail validation check, since we're allowing people to use either an e-mail address or a Web URL. This version of postmsg.cgi has been altered to disallow new posts, and also doesn't e-mail replies, so we've deleted the sendmail subroutine:

```perl
#!/usr/bin/perl -Tw
use strict;
use lib '.';
use MyBoard;
use HTML::TagFilter;

my($tf) = HTML::TagFilter->new;
# Now we're going to allow paragraph tags, breaks,
# italics, bolds, and links (<a href="whatever">)
$tf->allow_tags({p=>{'any'}}, {br=>{'any'}}, {i=>{'any'}},
{b=>{'any'}}, {a=>{'any'}});

# add a second TagFilter to remove ALL tags - use this
# on the e-mail address and subject line.
my($tf2) = HTML::TagFilter->new;
$tf2->allow_tags();

my($i, $sth, $asth, $rv, $replyto, $thread_id);

# do some error-checking - be sure they filled out all
# the fields
# $cgi->param returns an array of the input field names.
foreach $i ($cgi->param()) {
    if ($cgi->param($i) =~ /^\s*$/) {
        &dienice("$i was blank - please fill out all of the
fields.");
    }
}
my($subject) = $tf2->filter($cgi->param('subject'));
my($message) = $tf->filter($cgi->param('message'));
my($from) = $tf2->filter($cgi->param('name'));
my($email) = $tf2->filter($cgi->param('email'));
```

```
$sth = $dbh->prepare("insert into messages(author, subject,
email, date, ip, message, thread_id) values(?,?,?,
current_timestamp(),?,?,?)") or &dbdie;

# only allow it if it's a follow-up
if ($cgi->param('replyto_id') eq "") {
    &dienice("This shouldn't have happened, but you aren't
allowed to post new messages here - only follow-ups.");
} else {
    $asth = $dbh->prepare("select * from messages where id=?");
    $rv = $asth->execute($cgi->param('replyto_id'));
    $replyto = $asth->fetchrow_hashref;
    my($thread_id);
    if ($replyto->{'thread_id'} == 0) {
        $thread_id = $replyto->{'id'};
    } else {
        $thread_id = $replyto->{'thread_id'};
    }
    $sth->execute($from, $subject, $cgi->param('email'),
        $ENV{REMOTE_ADDR}, $message, $thread_id) or &dbdie;
    print $cgi->redirect("$url/message.cgi?$thread_id");
}
```

Source code: http://www.cgi101.com/advanced/blog/postmsg.txt

The Admin Area

Set up an admin directory for your blog just as you did for the forums (see Chapter 11).
The admin index.cgi will be shorter than the one for our forums, since there aren't any
forums to be created/edited/deleted. You just need to add links for posting new messages
and canceling messages. We're also adding a new script here to allow you to edit
existing messages.

index.cgi

```
#!/usr/bin/perl -wT
use strict;
use lib '../';
use MyBoard;
```

```
&do_header("$btitle Administration");
print qq(<h2>$btitle Administration</h2>\n);

print qq(<u><a href="newmsg.cgi">Post New
Message</a></u><p>\n<hr>\n);

# Cancel Messages
print <<EndCancel;
<form action="cancel.cgi" method="POST">
<u>Cancel Message</u> #:<input type="text" name="msgid" size=5>
<input type="submit" value="Cancel">
<font size=-1>You will be able to view the message and the IP
address it was posted from before canceling it.</font>
</form>
<hr>
EndCancel

# Edit Message
print <<EndEdit;
<form action="edit.cgi" method="POST">
<u>Edit Message</u> #:<input type="text" name="msgid" size=5>
<input type="submit" value="Edit">
</form>
<hr>
EndEdit

print qq(<p><a href="$url/">Back to $btitle</a></p>\n);

&do_footer;
```

Source code: http://www.cgi101.com/advanced/blog/adminindex.txt

newmsg.cgi

Again, this script is similar to the one in our forums code. We've moved it into the admin area so that only the blog owner can post *new* messages. And we've deleted any references to forums:

```
#!/usr/bin/perl -Tw
use strict;
use lib '../';
```

```
use MyBoard;

# declare variables
my($sth, $rv, $id, $name, $desc);

&do_header("New Topic in $btitle");

print <<EndForm;
<form action="postmsg.cgi" method="POST">
<pre>
Your Name:                  <input type="text" name="name" size=40
value="$ENV{REMOTE_USER}">
E-mail or Web Address: <input type="text" name="email" size=40>
Subject:                    <input type="text" name="subject"
size=40>
</pre>
Enter your message below. Please use HTML tags.<p>
<textarea name="message" rows=10 cols=78
wrap="HARD"></textarea>
<p>
<input type="submit" value="Post Message">
<input type="reset" value="Erase">
</form>

EndForm

&do_footer;
```

⊟ Source code: http://www.cgi101.com/advanced/blog/adminnewmsg.txt

If you're the only person posting blog entries, you may want to set the value= for your e-mail (or Web) address in the form as well, so you don't have to retype it every time you want to post a new message.

postmsg.cgi

Your blog will have two copies of postmsg.cgi - one in the main directory for posting replies, and this one in the admin area for posting new messages. We've removed any tag filtering or data validation from this copy, other than checking to be sure you didn't leave any fields blank. Presumably you won't be posting malicious HTML code to your own blog, so there's no reason to check for it.

```
#!/usr/bin/perl -Tw
use strict;
use lib '../';
use MyBoard;

my($i, $sth, $rv);

# do some error-checking - be sure they filled out all
# the fields
# $cgi->param returns an array of the input field names.
foreach $i ($cgi->param()) {
    if ($cgi->param($i) =~ /^\s*$/) {
        &dienice("$i was blank - please fill out all of the
fields.");
    }
}

$sth = $dbh->prepare("insert into messages(author, subject,
email, date, ip, message, thread_id) values(?,?,?,
current_timestamp(),?,?,?)") or &dbdie;

$sth->execute($cgi->param('name'), $cgi->param('subject'),
$cgi->param('email'), $ENV{REMOTE_ADDR}, $cgi->param('message'),
0) or &dbdie;

print $cgi->redirect("$url");
```

Source code: http://www.cgi101.com/advanced/blog/adminpostmsg.txt

cancel.cgi

This script can be copied from the forums admin area (see Chapter 13). The only line
that needs changing is the initial database query:

```
$sth = $dbh->prepare("select messages.*,
date_format(date,'%c/%e/%Y %r') as
nicedate, forums.name from messages, forums where
messages.forum = forums.id and (messages.id=? or thread_id=?)
order by thread_id, date") or &dbdie;
```

now becomes:

```
$sth = $dbh->prepare("select messages.*,
date_format(date,'%c/%e/%Y %r') as
nicedate from messages where (messages.id=? or thread_id=?)
order by
thread_id, date") or &dbdie;
```

We've removed the references to the forums table. The cancel2.cgi script can be copied directly from the forums admin directory, and needs no changes.

⊟ Source code: http://www.cgi101.com/advanced/blog/admincancel.txt
⊟ Source code: http://www.cgi101.com/advanced/blog/admincancel2.txt

edit.cgi

You might want to edit something in a blog entry you've already posted, and changing it manually using MySQL is not very convenient. Here's a script to let you edit existing entries.

```
#!/usr/bin/perl -Tw
use strict;
use lib '../';
use MyBoard;

my($msgid, $sth, $rv, $msg, $resp);

# untaint the message number
# this is different from message.cgi in that it's a
# posted value rather than the query string.
if ($cgi->param('msgid') =~ /^(\d+)$/) {
    $msgid = $1;
} else {
    &dienice($cgi->param('msgid') . " isn't a valid message
number.");
}

$sth = $dbh->prepare("select * from messages where id=?") or
&dbdie;
$rv = $sth->execute($msgid);
if ($rv < 1) {
    &dienice("Message ID $msgid doesn't exist.");
```

```
}
$msg = $sth->fetchrow_hashref;

&do_header("Edit Message");

my($message) = &detag($msg->{message});

print <<EndHTML;
<form action="edit2.cgi" method="POST">
<input type="hidden" name="msgid" value="$msgid">
<b>Subject:</b> $msg->{subject}<p>
<b>Message:</b><br>
<textarea name="message" rows=10 cols=78>
$message </textarea><p>
<input type="submit" value="Save Changes">
</form>
EndHTML

&do_footer;

sub detag {
    my($str) = @_;
    $str =~ s/&/&amp;/g;
    $str =~ s/</&lt;/g;
    $str =~ s/>/&gt;/g;
    return $str;
}
```

⊡ Source code: http://www.cgi101.com/advanced/blog/adminedit.txt

Notice we've added a detag subroutine here; this converts HTML tags into HTML
entities. If you don't convert these, your browser will display the marked-up text in the
form input field, and the tags will be lost as soon as you click "Save". "&" is converted
to & (the HTML entity for ampersand); "<" is converted to < (the HTML entity
for less-than), and ">" is converted to > (the HTML entity for greater-than). It's
important to convert the ampersands *first*, or else you'll end up turning your > and
< tags into &gt; and &lt;, which aren't useful and will destroy your
existing tags.

Finally, edit2.cgi takes the edited data and replaces the data in the database:

```perl
#!/usr/bin/perl -Tw
use strict;
use lib '../';
use MyBoard;

my($sth,$rv,$msgid);

$msgid = $cgi->param('msgid');

$sth = $dbh->prepare("update messages set message=? where
id=?");
$rv = $sth->execute($cgi->param('message'), $msgid);

print $cgi->redirect("$url/message.cgi?$msgid");
```

⊟ Source code: http://www.cgi101.com/advanced/blog/adminedit2.txt

This example only allows you to edit the actual message; if you want to be able to edit the subject, author or e-mail address, just add a field for those to the input form and adjust your MySQL update query accordingly.

That completes the blog code. While this is a short and simple example of a blog, the scripts are easily modifiable to add whatever advanced features you want.

Index

CGI101.COM Web Hosting

If you need a place to test, develop, and/or host your message board program, blog, or other CGI programs, CGI 101.COM can help. We offer CGI-friendly Unix shell and virtual hosting Web accounts, all of which include:

- Several programming languages, including Perl, Java, C, C++, and TCL (and we'll install others, if needed)
- A variety of pre-installed Perl modules, including the popular CGI and LWP modules for Web-related programming, GD for creating graphics on the fly, and many others
- A library of ready-to-use CGI scripts, including guestbooks, form-mailers, counters, ad banners, and more
- PHP and Server-Side Includes
- MySQL
- Use of our secure server (https://secure.cgi101.com/~yourusername/)
- The mod_auth_mysql module, which allows you to create password-protected directories that look up username/password info from a MySQL database
- procmail, for powerful mail processing and filtering
- A free subscription to WebTemplates, a collection of ready-made Web page templates you can use to build your new Website, right from your browser
- Nightly tape backups
- Web-based E-mail, quota checking, and account information panel
- Spam filtering with SpamAssassin can block most spam e-mail you receive, so you never even have to see it
- Virus blocking at our mail server keeps most viruses from ending up in your inbox

Visit http://www.cgi101.com/hosting/ to sign up for an account!